RAISING AN
Original

We love this book! Julie has given every parent an incredible gift—to see through the eyes of their child. It's revolutionary. You won't be the same parent after you read this fantastic book and use the proven personality tool.

DRS. LES & LESLIE PARROTT, No. 1 *New York Times* bestseller authors of *Saving Your Marriage Before It Starts*

In the age of political correctness there is supreme importance placed on normality. For parents, there is a very real temptation to produce cookie-cutter kids who don't stand out and do not stand up for truth. *Raising an Original* highlights a critical point, that your child is a unique image-bearer of the Almighty, and it is this originality that should be celebrated and nurtured. If you want to raise children that desire to glorify God by unabashedly reflecting his distinctiveness, buy this book.

DR. JOSHUA MYERS, Operations Director and Clinical Counselor at the Timothy Center, Instructor of Psychology at Liberty University, and cohost of Pairadocs Podcast

Julie's message of your unique calling to raise your one-of-a-kind child is one every parent needs to hear. You will finish it feeling confident and purposeful and up for the task.

NATALIE HANSON, wife to Taylor Hanson, mother of five, writer and blogger at http://natonthewall.com

What I loved about *Raising an Original* is that is wasn't written by an ivory-tower member of academia, it was written by a mom. And not just any mom, a mom of eight. Wisdom flows effortlessly from every page from a woman that has walked in the steps of her Savior with her children and had the brilliance to stop and write down all that she has learned. In a time when we fear that our kids are going to end up looking like all their secular peers at school, *Raising an Original* is a God-breathed love letter to your family.

DR. JIMMY MYERS, LPC-S, Marriage and Family
Therapist Executive Director of the Timothy
Center and author of *Toe to Toe With Your Teen*

RAISING AN *Original*

PARENTING EACH CHILD ACCORDING TO THEIR UNIQUE GOD-GIVEN TEMPERAMENT

JULIE LYLES CARR

Z ZONDERVAN®

ZONDERVAN

Raising an Original
Copyright © 2016 by Julie Lyles Carr

Requests for information should be addressed to:
Zondervan, 3900 *Sparks Dr. SE, Grand Rapids, Michigan* 49546

ISBN 978-0-310-34590-9 (ebook)

Library of Congress Cataloging-in-Publication Data

Names: Carr, Julie Lyles, author.
Title: Raising an original : parenting each child according to their unique God-given
    temperament / Julie Lyles Carr.
Description: Grand Rapids : Zondervan, 2016.
Identifiers: LCCN 2016005822 | ISBN 9780310345893 (softcover)
Subjects: LCSH: Parenting—Religious aspects—Christianity. | Child rearing—Religious
    aspects—Christianity. | Temperament—Religious aspects—Christianity.
Classification: LCC BV4529 .C426 2016 | DDC 248.8/45—dc23 LC record available at
    https://lccn.loc.gov/2016005822

Cover design: *Micah Kandros*
Cover photo: © *Sunny studio / Shutterstock*
Interior design: *Kait Lamphere*

First printing July 2016 / Printed in the United States of America

For Michael.
You've always believed.
For my father,
Bob Lyles.
I heard you, Daddy. I heard you.

CONTENTS

Foreword by Randy Phillips. 11

PART 1 *The Weaving of an Original Life:*
Beautiful, Curious Threads 13

    1 Someone Original to Raise. 15

    2 The Original Mission. 33

PART 2 *The Ties That Tangle: Avoiding Parenting Pitfalls* . . . 51

    3 It's Not Just about Finding Them That Job 53

    4 It's Not Just about Getting Them That Degree . . . 71

    5 It's Not Just about Protecting Them 88

    6 And It's Not about You. 107

PART 3 *Tools for the Trade:* **Raising an Original**
Personality Evaluation Summary 125

    7 Learning the ROPES—Discovering Your
       Child's Personality Style. 127

    8 Practicing the ROPES—Nurturing Your
       Child's Original Style. 153

PART 4 *Living Original* 177

    9 On Overload Mode—Evaluating
        the Extracurricular. 179
    10 Purposed, Not Perfect 205
    11 Originals Given Back to the Originator 222

PART 5 *The Launch*. 235

    12 An Original Legacy 237

    Acknowledgments. 249
    Notes. 253

FOREWORD BY RANDY PHILLIPS

THE LONGER I'm in ministry, the more people I meet, the more songs I sing, the more years that tick by, there is an area of life that seems to grow more mysterious and more beautiful and more complex. Parenting.

From being a father to my two girls, Garland and Lily, to interacting with the families in our church and music ministry, I find there's nothing like being a parent to challenge you, test you, grow you, and at times completely bewilder you. I want to do right by my kids, and most importantly, I want my kids to be everything God intends them to be. We can get caught up in looking for some ideal, one-size-fits-all approach when it comes to child raising. But as most parents know, our kids are unique and different from each other. I know that what worked for Denise and me in raising Garland hasn't always connected with Lily in the same way. Different girls, different gifts, different hearts, different needs. Unique lyrics with distinct melodies, both of them stunning songs of God's creativity, these two daughters of mine.

That's what's so exciting about *Raising an Original*. You'll be challenged to reconsider the goal of your parenting. And you'll be equipped with innovative tools to learn who your kids really are, how God individually designs each child, and how that individuality can be nurtured and guided. Most importantly, you'll learn how to cooperate with God in the spectacular unfolding of the story of your child's life and purpose in the kingdom.

As Julie Lyles Carr's pastor, I can tell you this: she is always the smartest person in the room! Pay close attention to her words and wisdom. I know I do. Whether she is teaching, preaching, writing, blogging, managing, or parenting eight kids, everything she does is with amazing excellence and bathed in prayer. *Raising an Original* will absolutely stun you with its truths about and insights into parenting. Dive into this book not only for yourself but for the legacy that will outlive you. Well done, Julie!

Randy Phillips, lead pastor, LifeAustin;
founder of Phillips Craig & Dean

PART 1

THE WEAVING OF AN ORIGINAL LIFE:

Beautiful, Curious Threads

CHAPTER 1

SOMEONE ORIGINAL TO RAISE

*Parents are like shuttles on a loom. They join
the threads of the past with threads of the future
and leave their own bright patterns as they go.*

Fred Rogers

HER AMBITIONS had been so much higher.

And humbler, in a sense.

Zélie had wanted to give her life to the Church, to devote herself to good works and prayer and contemplation.

But the Sisters of Charity of Saint Vincent de Paul turned Marie-Azélie Guérin (Zélie to her family) away, sending her packing because of her lingering asthma and debilitating migraines. She was dispatched back to her tiny hometown, the shards of her dreams making for wincing steps.

In the depths of a pool of disappointment, she found a new prayer, a new request. If she was not to be a bride of the Church, then she asked to become the bride of a man and to bear children fully consecrated to God.

Then there came a period of waiting, the pause between prayer and reply. Zélie moved to the capital city of the region, picking up training in the local textile market. The artisans of the city had developed a unique industry, one that transformed the common into the choice, the drab into the dazzling. They were sculptors of string, weavers of whimsy. Zélie learned their art quickly and with great skill.

She became a lacemaker.

Lace. That froth of thread that embellishes, that raises the value of cloth, the finishing garnish of cuff and hem and seam. In that day, no place was more renowned for its lace than Alençon, France, the city Zélie now called home. She mastered the art of point d'Alençon lace, and her work became famous throughout France. She even opened her own shop on Rue Saint-Blaise.

Alençon was also the home of Louis Martin, the watchmaker.

They met in 1858—the lacemaker and the watchmaker—and fell in love.

She became Zélie Martin, wife of the watchmaker. And Louis and Zélie, in time, became parents. Of the nine babies Zélie birthed, five survived to adulthood. All daughters. And all went into the service of the Church, consecrated to God. Just as their mother had prayed.

Zélie the lacemaker. Her original pious plan had been replaced by wielding a thread, running a business, and raising a generation. She created a legacy that exponentially impacted—to a factor of five—the Church she so loved.

In the weaving of her daughters' childhoods, what was it that Zélie the lacemaker wove into the lives of her five diverse daughters? How did she curate the curious threads of five individuals who had been placed into her lacemaking hands? How did she knit such purpose and passion into the very fabric of her children's characters?

Completely befuddled. And blissful.

For the first time in many, many years, I was sitting on an airplane by myself. That was the befuddled part.

By myself—that was the blissful part. Alone. Except for the other passengers.

I wouldn't even look at my row mate. Not a glance. Not a glimpse.

We sat a mere eighteen inches apart, and courtesy dictated that I would ask her an obligatory question or two, expressing at least a sprinkling of mild interest.

But no. I had made a promise to myself. I would allow myself to be alone.

I was flying to Paris, and I was determined to embrace the quiet. Alone.

As a mom of eight children, *alone* and *quiet* are generally not experiences I have. My daily life is a blessed blizzard of shouts and laughter and mud and mess and intrusion and needs and joy and fatigue. It's amazing and exhausting and never, ever boring.

Or quiet.

Or solitary.

Hence that promise to myself when I boarded the plane. Thankfully, my row mate also seemed to have little interest in chatting. We made flickering eye contact and exchanged slight smiles as she passed me my dinner somewhere over the Atlantic, but we then returned to honoring our unspoken vow of silence.

Bliss.

Just before we landed, my Southern genes won out and I turned to her, apologizing for my antisocial Atlantic crossing. I explained that this was the first time in a long time that I'd been away from kids and home and work, and I was soaking up the solitude. She laughed and said that she too was a busy mom, grateful for the nine hours of quiet we had silently gifted each other.

When we landed, jet lagged and happy, I ran into the arms of my oldest daughter, Madison, who was spending the year in Paris studying at the Sorbonne and nannying for a French family. Walking into the crisp air of a glorious Paris morning, we inhaled brioche before heading to the Champs-Élysées.

Not my usual daily routine of Cheerios sticking to my bare feet as I navigated a trashed kitchen in search of day-old yet life-sustaining coffee.

Because of her nanny schedule, Madison had to work several hours each afternoon during my five-day visit, so I found myself with another unexpected gift—quiet hours to roam La Ville Lumière, the City of Light. During this time I made my way to the Louvre, slowly drinking it all in. I observed the Mona Lisa, serene despite the crowd surging into her gallery. I took in the majestic Winged Victory, the Egyptian exhibits. I ambled through gallery after gallery, no agenda, no hurry.

Drawn to a quiet wing of the retired palace, I found myself in a suite of chambers away from the crush of tourists. No noise of crowds. No flashing of cameras.

And that's where I met another lacemaker.

Johannes Vermeer had painted her likeness, dipping his brush into a kaleidoscope of pigment, capturing her image just as her needle was about to again wind through the thread, creating a delicate web.

La Dentellière. That's what the French call her. *The Lacemaker.*

I stood transfixed for a long time, taking in Vermeer's work. Known as one of the Dutch masters, Vermeer worked in Delft of the Dutch Netherlands in the mid-1600s. Not well-known in his own time, he was a tired father of fifteen children, juggling the responsibility of feeding many mouths with the need to keep himself supplied in paints and brushes. His genius is in the seeming simplicity of his work. The background is bare, the canvas very small, the subject performing a simple task with simple tools. Her head is bowed over her work in quiet intensity, skeins of red and blue thread resting on a small table as her hands go about their job. No fanfare. No razzle-dazzle.

I stood there, fixated, trying to decide what it was about this particular painting that drew me so strongly.

Hormones, maybe. I did a quick calendar calculation. Yeah, maybe a little sentimental PMS.

Finally, I decided it would be bad form to spend the entire afternoon in front of just one painting. It might make the other artists jealous. I pulled away and continued my tour, scouting more of the collections and reflecting as I strolled. But I continued to ponder the diminutive wonder of La Dentellière.

Eventually she drew me back. I just had to go stand before the lacemaker one more time. There she was, still intent on her work, still mesmerizing.

So I did what any self-respecting American would do. I pulled out my camera and captured her for myself. Flash off, thank you very much. No judging.

The rest of my days in Paris with my oldest child were wonderful and restful and sweet. We ate macaroons and went to Versailles, and I ran some miles in the Tuileries Gardens. All too soon, it was time to return stateside.

La Dentellière continued to fascinate me, even after arriving back on Texas soil. What was it about her? I scoured for information on Vermeer, thinking perhaps La Dentellière had some exciting mystery about her.

Nope. Nothing.

Going back through my pictures from the trip, it finally dawned on me.

La Dentellière seemed a perfect metaphor of parenting.

THE CURIOUS THREAD

We all begin life on a fragile string.

A thread—a life-sustaining, nutrient-giving thread. This thread connects the fragile to the established, the dependent to the provider.

A curious thread.

About twenty inches long and three-quarters of an inch in diameter, the umbilical cord is the literal lifeline between mother and child, the circulatory cable that allows life to exist in darkened maternal seclusion.

A marvelous, miraculous, curious thread, ingeniously designed.

And, ultimately, a thread that must be cut.

Cut so that other curious threads woven into an individual person may begin to flourish. Separate. Unwoven from the connection to the womb. Then to be woven again by the influence of a parent, the empowering, the potentially tangling, the threads of possibility gleaming throughout. Woven into the destiny of an individual.

These curious threads run through all of us, strands of personality and possibility and purpose that are present from the very inception of our lives. Some of us grab hold of those threads and weave together a lace of life that reflects all we were meant to be. Others never quite learn to grasp them, leaving the hems of their lives unfinished and ragged, dangling strings where a fabric of purpose could have been.

Once that curious thread of the umbilical cord is cut, we parents are handed a wet, warm bundle of human along with brief instructions on feeding and diaper changing.

But what about the lacemaking of a little one's life? What about the weaving of beautiful threads into a delicate web of destiny and character that adorns a heart dedicated to God?

EACH AN ORIGINAL

Zélie Martin understood thread. She understood weaving. She understood the skill and delicacy needed to render beauty and artistry from disconnected strands.

She also understood children. She wrote of her daughters' unique dispositions, the singularities of their spirits. She appeared to approach their upbringings much as she did her vocational skill, with tenderness and intentionality and a view to the completed piece.

Vermeer's La Dentellière, his lacemaker, has helped me see the power of parenting that is built on discovering and weaving with purpose the gorgeous strands God has placed in these children with whom He entrusts us. To take fascinating fibers of enormous potential, to focus intently, to keep the background distraction to a minimum, and to weave.

As parents, we are weaving tabernacles for the soul. Exodus 35:25 says, "All the women skilled at weaving brought their weavings of blue and purple and scarlet fabrics and their fine linens. And all the women who were gifted in spinning, spun the goats' hair" (MSG).

These ancient artisans created the very coverings that housed the presence of God in the desert. Today, our mandate remains the same. We are tasked with taking threads of life in our children and helping shape them as a dwelling for the Spirit of God. King Lemuel's mother, talking about a woman of valor in Proverbs 31:13, was speaking of cloth making when she said, "She seeks wool and flax, and works with willing hands [to develop it]" (ESV). But it seems to me she was on to something deeper as well.

There is an intentionality in the weaving, a respect of the fibers of a being. From our very conception, the weaving begins.

Deoxyribonucleic acid. DNA. The stuff we're woven of.

Scientists tell us our composition is of strands, cords, strings of DNA. To our very molecular makeup, we are threads of design. Within our DNA we carry the building blocks of a human. But God also leaves enough wiggle room to ensure that no two individuals are exactly alike. Even identical twins have subtle differences. God builds into the human experience an incredible foundational truth: We are all, each of us, an original. The Divine Lacemaker gathers His similar threads for life and weaves them anew for every human brought to existence. And when He makes us parents, He invites us to participate in that miraculous process, the process He began back in a garden.

GARDEN DREAMS

Hydrangeas the size of basketballs. Petunias with faces as broad as saucers. Vegetables bursting with flavor and hue.

My grandmother could grow anything.

Many summers of my childhood, we would make the long trek from Southern California to the Mississippi Delta to visit my extended family. We always knew right away when we'd arrived at Grandmother Lyles's house. Not because the house itself was remarkable. It wasn't.

It was the cacophony of living color in the flowerbeds, the trailing floral vines that gave curve and dimension to the cyclone fence. The geometry of the rectangular vegetable garden, plants reaching for the sky, ranks standing in precise rows. Tomatoes, fat with scarlet cheekiness, lounged over the rungs of their silver cages, unaware of their upcoming fate—to be dredged in cornmeal and baptized in sizzling shortening, surrendering their flavors of soil and sunshine. Green beans, bow-tied with twine, invited us to pluck them from their vines. I remember sitting at my grandmother's small table with her, learning the art of snapping beans into precise one-inch chunks with a percussive rhythm.

Gardening seemed the simplest endeavor as I watched my grandmother pick her flowers and harvest her vegetables.

When Michael and I had been married for a few years, we built our first little house. From the forest green tile in the tiny entry to the black marble countertops in the master bath, I made bold—and sometimes regrettable—decisions on the finishings. I had a vision of what I wanted this little house to be, and that vision included flowerbeds and a garden that would make Grandmother Lyles proud.

I initially set out to carve flowerbeds along the front of the house, spade in hand. Discovery number one: Digging up sod is not easy. As in, extremely not easy. I called for reinforcements, and Michael and I struggled and shoveled and raked. What I had thought would be a thirty-minute flowerbed prep required far more time—with nothing to show for it.

Discovery number two: Prepping flowerbeds is a muddy, messy business. Cute pink gardening gloves morphed into ragged, blackened mitts. Rain transformed the freshly turned soil into a mucky swamp. The mud-encrusted shoes we piled by the front door after each shoveling session were not in keeping with my imagination's vision of gleaming garden wellies and quirky watering pail.

Once the flowerbed was marked out, albeit with a wobbly border, it was time to head for the local home-and-garden superstore and purchase loads of flowers. True, we'd had a few setbacks, but we were nearing the finish. We'd bring home a truckload of flowers and shrubs, plant them in the ground, and *voila!*—a flower garden like my grandmother's.

Except.

Flowers were expensive. Shrubbery was astronomical. I kept

thinking there must be some kind of mistake. How could a little twig, practically bent over from the weight of the price tag, be worth that much? My vision was going to require some serious editing. On our tiny budget, we could only afford a few six-packs of meager blooms—anemic little red-and-white striped petunias. But I was certain that once we got those plants in the ground, they would fill in the border nicely.

About the same time, undaunted, we also decided to start a vegetable garden. We'd learned a bit from the flowerbed preparation, so we drafted a friend to help us out this time. Together, we carved a huge rectangle in a corner of our little backyard, marking the perimeter with railroad ties pungent with the scent of tar. It was an impressive rectangle. An empty, soil-turned rectangle. But a fairly congruous rectangle. Progress!

I briefly turned my attention back to the front flowerbed and popped a few dozen of the little petunias into the ground. Well, now. Petunias don't go far, even once you've released them from their plastic containers. My flower garden was not lush. It was not dense. The entire collection filled only a sliver of the bed, blooms crammed to one end of the naked, raw earth. *Hmmm.* I made some adjustments, spreading them out a bit more. Even less lush and less dense, but at least we had flowers. Sorta progress.

The encouraging news for the backyard garden was that seed packets were eminently more affordable than actual plants. We stocked up on paper envelopes of plant potential, snagging both the familiar and the exotic—beans, squash, eggplant, carrots, radishes, onions. It didn't matter if it was something our family would typically eat or not. The bounteous pictures on the front of the seed packets held such promise! I imagined our harvest display on the butcher-block farm table in our tiny kitchen, a rustic basket overflowing with dewy produce. "Oh, that," I would say, all casual and smug. "That's from our garden. Why, yes, we grew it ourselves." My visitors would be so impressed and—possibly, hopefully—a little envious. In a Christian kind of way.

We gave the instructions on the backs of the seed packets a capricious perusal, poked holes in the ground, and dropped in seeds. We may have lost track of what got planted where, but assumed we could figure it out once seedlings started pushing up through the ground. I mean, a zucchini looks like a zucchini, right? Rinsing our hands and knocking the mud off our shoes, we stood back to admire our work. Now all that remained was to enjoy the yield.

For a while, I found great delight in watering our flowerbed and garden. It seemed almost meditative, swirling my wrist— spray nozzle in hand—and making arcs of water in the sunlight. But then I had to water the next day. And the next. And it was getting hotter as summer progressed. And it was getting a little boring. And then I forgot to water for a day or two . . . or four.

In the front flowerbed, the red-and-white striped petunias were struggling. They were supposed to complement the Cape Cod-gray paint of our siding and the weathered red brick exterior of the house, but they seemed to lack ambition for the job. They bowed near to the ground, refusing to perk up.

Green shoots started to appear in the backyard garden. Inexplicably, though, they all looked the same. I would gaze with pride at a robust seedling reaching toward the sun, only to discover the next day what I'd thought was an exotic lettuce was actually a dandelion. Or I would weed out a sprig of Bermuda grass only to discover an onion attached to its root.

And then there was the mystery of why some patches of ground were oddly bare and others were crammed with greenery. Beyond that, the produce that *was* showing up wasn't cooperating with the color palette of my imagined tablescape. Squash was appearing everywhere. Yellow, yellow, and more yellow. We'd pull it out, but more would appear within hours.

What about the purple of the eggplant? The red of the tomato? The green of the broccoli? The eggplant never did appear. The tomatoes looked like tiny, red, shriveled berries. And the broccoli seemed like it wasn't going to be ready anytime soon. So the tablescape stayed yellow, yellow, yellow—squash yellow. It was the kind of squash yield you shared with all the neighbors. At first, they were grateful. Then they were accommodating. Then they stopped answering the door.

By the end of the gardening season, we'd managed two quasi-bumper crops—the overachieving squash and bitter, peppery radishes that made your eyes water and your sinuses release. For reasons still mysterious to us, our second daughter, McKenna, would lie in the sunshine and dirt, eating those grimy radishes with great abandon. The mosquitoes left her alone that year. Go figure.

What on earth had happened? I was the granddaughter of a green thumb who made gardening seem effortless. Other people were able to curate hearty landscapes without too much trouble. And look at the forests and meadows! Things seemed to grow in nature just fine, and no one was there wringing her hands over it. So why had our flora been such a flop?

ONE OF A KIND

When I talk with other parents—and when I take a look at my own heart—I realize we all have one thing in common: We don't want our kids to flop.

Some of us stumble into parenthood and others plan their parenting path with precise rigor. Some start college funds before the baby is even born and others remember last-minute to register their kid for kindergarten. Some of us feel well-prepared for motherhood and fatherhood, and others change their very first diaper ever when the new baby comes home. Regardless of the preparation we've had, the advice we've received, and the attitude we bring to the endeavor, there's one thing upon which the whole deal revolves.

Your child is a one-of-a-kind.

Nobody has ever raised your kid before.

Parenting is a real-time experience. A learning-on-the-job scenario. You can never completely prepare for it.

You can have reams of resources on how to raise a child—and much of it can be valuable. But there's always one deficit.

There's no manual on how to raise *your* kid. Because no one has done it before.

You've been invited by God to participate in a truly singular event—the upbringing of a person who has never before existed,

> **NOBODY HAS EVER RAISED YOUR KID BEFORE.**

someone with a fresh blend of characteristics, gifts, and purpose. A new life with a new offering for the world. A soul set in this season with a specificity of God's intent.

When the Apostle Paul was visiting Athens, he spoke at the Areopagus, a meeting place for the leading thinkers and philosophers of the day. In an ancient TED Talk, Paul told the people, "From one man he made all the nations, that they should inhabit the whole earth; and he marked out their appointed times in history and the boundaries of their lands. God did this so that they would seek him and perhaps reach out for him and find him, though he is not far from any one of us. 'For in him we live and move and have our being'" (Acts 17:26–28).

God has thought everything out and created us and placed us

in exactly the era in which He intended. You. Me. Your spouse. Your child. Even your grumpy neighbor. As the prolific songwriter David penned, ". . . all the days ordained for me were written in your book before one of them came to be" (Psalm 139:16).

God has sent your child into your arms and into your home and your heart for a reason and for a season. Whether your child is a challenge or a charm, an easy-going peacemaker or a complex essence, God has imbued him or her to be a presence in this generation, in this culture, in this epoch. And He appointed you as that child's parent. That child's guide. That child's coach and cheerleader and advocate and disciplinarian. To do those jobs well, you're going to need to know your child—his personality, his challenges, the unique strands that went into the knitting of him. You're not just going to need to know popular philosophies of childrearing.

You're raising an original.

And that's going to take an original approach.

KNOWING WHAT WORKS

Back to my garden.

Back to that experience which started with such high expectations and lofty goals and ended with a rather baffling—not to mention disappointing—aftermath.

If good intentions had been enough, if high expectations had sufficed, everything should have bloomed. But we missed a few critical pieces. We placed our plans, our opinions, our preferences, our vision of what we wanted our yard and garden to look like, over a few important essentials and, in doing so, we missed out on seeing things flourish the way they could have.

We're barely into chapter 2 of God's autobiography when we

find Him out gardening. Genesis 2 says, "Now the Lord God had planted a garden in the east, in Eden; and there he put the man he had formed. The Lord God made all kinds of trees grow out of the ground—trees that were pleasing to the eye and good for food. . . . A river watering the garden flowed from Eden" (Genesis 2:8–10). In those few verses lie some deep insight into how God designed His creation's system.

Everything Has Certain Conditions in Which It Thrives

We can have a grand plan of where we want to place things, what we think would look good where.

And then there's what comes designed into that plant, that creature, that life.

Those red-and-white striped petunias? The ones that looked straggly and viney, not full and opulent? I had planted them on the side of the house that received minimal sunlight. Petunias are designed to flourish in full sunshine, as many hours a day as possible. In my desire to have their boisterous color accent the hue of my house, I'd put them in a place where, regardless of my watering and worrying, they could not thrive.

And in the backyard garden, where we'd thrown everything into full sun? You guessed it. We'd planted some things that needed the benefit of at least a little shade. We'd also watered everything at the same rate, which was terrific for a few plants, tolerated by others, and terrible for some.

What worked for one plant didn't work for them all.

Timing and Season Matter

We'd planted everything in the spring because spring is planting time, right? Not always. Depending on the plant, it may thrive better in earlier or later seasons. Some plants grow better when they're cultivated closer to autumn. Or they may grow healthier roots if planted just as winter angles toward spring. Things weren't going to bloom on my timetable, regardless of how much I needed the purple of an eggplant to offset the yellow of the squash.

The Condition of the Soil Makes a Massive Difference

I don't know what kind of dirt we had in our first garden. All I knew is that it was dirt. But plants require a variety of nutrients from the soil in which they're planted. Some need more alkaline soil, some more acidic. The ideal loam for flowers is different from what green beans require. Some plants don't require much in the way of terra firma, while others need an entourage of high-end earth.

After our garden flop, I recalled Grandmother Lyles's interesting practices with her crops. While making a meal, she would reserve eggshells, coffee grounds, and fish innards. After dinner, she would make the rounds in her garden, placing a bit of this here and a bit of that there. I suppose at the time I thought it was some kind of odd garbage-and-fish-guts burial ritual. What she was actually doing, though, was supplementing and strengthening the soil for each of her individual plants. Just because her hydrangeas flourished in one kind of soil didn't mean it was suitable for roses.

It Takes a While

We wanted to pop our little plants and seeds into the ground, sprinkle some water on them, and experience a hasty harvest. But growth takes time. And repetition. And patience. The trick isn't in the initial actions of framing and planting. It's in the abiding, the remaining, the nurturing and weeding and trimming and pruning. And then, after a while—after a good, long while—planting flowers.

Our parenting journeys are a lot like gardening. They're also a lot like lacemaking. We want to weave something of the threads of life that come with each child. We decide to start a family. We think about how fulfilling it will be to have a family portrait filled with cute kids. We plan the nursery, stop the birth control, fill out the adoption papers, choose a season of life, and dig in.

And then these little creatures arrive in our lives.

They bring with them personality and purpose and strength and challenges, woven into a squalling bundle that isn't too impressed with all our expectation. That cute schedule we printed out and laminated? It never met the baby with some serious colic. Our rigid ideas about nap time? They're sidelined by a cheerful soul who doesn't believe in—or need—much shut-eye.

This is the opening act of what will be several decades of learning and uncovering and discovering exactly who these little people are that God has placed in our lives. Your child will zoom ahead of the charts in some areas and may lag behind in others. Her timing and her season are specific to *her*—as well as the atmosphere of your home, the foundation of your faith walk, the state of your marriage, the personalities of her siblings. All of these contribute to the discovering, the nurturing, the connecting, the guiding, and, ultimately, the launching of your child into God's purpose for her.

It's going to take intentionality.

It's going to take letting go of presuppositions.

It's going to take being aware of potential tangles.

It's going to take discovering new tools and learning how to use them.

It's going to take being aware of and being honest about who you are and how the truth of that intersects with who your child is.

It's going to take time and attention and maturity and love.

It's going to take prayer. A lot of prayer.

And coffee.

Now is the best time to begin, no matter if you're waiting for your due date or up waiting for your teen to get home from a date.

Let's wake up to the presumptions and assumptions that may be influencing our parenting in ways that don't honor raising an original. Let's create a fresh standard. And let's equip ourselves to seek and recognize the incredible, curious threads in our children.

Notice the nuances.

Enhance the extraordinary.

Coach the calling.

Your child is here for a God purpose. You are here to parent that purpose. So saddle up and pick your metaphor. We've got some weaving to do. Some framing to create. Some gardening that awaits.

Someone original to raise.

CHAPTER 2

THE ORIGINAL MISSION

Well, as far as I'm concerned, I'm not here to
live a normal life. I'm sent here on a mission.
Howard Finster

98.6 DEGREES Fahrenheit.

Normal human body temperature.

You can thank Dr. Carl Reinhold August Wunderlich for
that number. In the mid-1800s, he took underarm temperature
readings on thousands of volunteers, utilizing a brand-new technology known as the mercury thermometer. He diligently took
reading after reading, recording each temperature, noting the
volunteer and the time of day. After he'd collected readings on
25,000 volunteers, Dr. Wunderlich began some serious number
crunching (sans calculator). He came up with 98.6 degrees as the
average human body temperature.

That number has stood as the standard for over 150 years. But
in 2005, researchers decided to take a fresh look at that Fahrenheit
familiar. Dear Dr. Wunderlich's thermometer was examined.
And found wanting.

It turns out that the mercury wand that had been used to take
so many temperature readings was off. All of Dr. Wunderlich's
careful computations, all those nights of adding up long columns
of numbers—wrong.

Bummer.

So we're left to ask, what's normal anyway?

If a standard for "normal" human body temperature has stood for a century and a half and we're just now questioning it, what other "normal" things might be off?

Bell curves. Growth and development charts. Report cards. Test scores. The neighbor's kid. All barometers for measuring our children. Eager to reassure ourselves that our kids are doing okay, have we taken time to make sure the things we're using to establish "normal" are correctly calibrated to our primary mission as parents?

And are we actually clear on what that primary mission is, anyway?

Many of us have a sense that our general mission is to raise children who love and worship God and are upstanding, moral citizens.

But the world's definition of *success* can creep in to that mission, adding layer upon layer to our perceived responsibilities. Of course, that's not all bad. Education, activities, hobbies, and friends add color and texture to our lives. But our culture has a way of shifting and shaping itself. The goals that are lifted up as measures of success today will look different tomorrow. And we need to parent our kids on the bedrock principle that God places plans and purposes—not trends, curves, and drifts—for His kids.

THE REAL MISSION

I need a show of hands here.

Don't be embarrassed.

Just quietly slip your hand up if these next two words mean something significant to you.

Duran Duran.

That's what I thought. I am not alone.

A lot of us who are parents now were in high school in the '80s and '90s. When I look back at my high school yearbooks and my scrapbooks from college, I often hear some serious giggling going on over my shoulder. My kids will drape themselves over me, viewing the annals of my history as fodder for high comedy.

We all thought we looked pretty good in those shoulder pads and pegged jeans, big permed hair and plastic earrings the size of teacup saucers. Right? To be "normal," you needed to have that look. To be "normal," you needed to act a certain way and talk a certain way and wear certain things. Social success was based on achieving those norms.

And now my kids are wearing my high school and college leftovers to costume parties.

I only bring up my unfortunate fashion past to make a point: Some of the things we find so important in the moment—things that we believe define *success* and *accomplishment* and *having arrived*—end up not being of eternal consequence.

Including Forenza sweaters.

Likewise, we need to be mindful of the trends we're bringing to our parenting wardrobes, what expectations we're draping over our families. When I speak with young moms in my teaching and mentoring ministry, I find our conversations are all about nursing or bottle-feeding, co-sleeping or cribs, slings or strollers, epidurals or natural childbirth. When I speak with mothers of toddlers and early elementary children, we hash through developmental stages, temper tantrums, and discipline. And with moms of older kids, we chat about academics and extracurricular activities, scholarships and proms.

All timely conversations for important stages. We *need* support and advice to get us through childhood challenges.

But these stages only mark points on the timeline up to when kids need to take wing and fly. And I find, for the most part, we're talking mainly about temporal issues. Not character. Not purpose.

We're chatting it up about shoulder pads when we should be talking about robes of righteousness and mantles of meaning. We should be looking at lacemaking, at the weaving of curious threads. We should be talking about raising originals who don't have to be squished into the outlines of a fickle culture with its wavering definitions of what's normal.

Here's the real mission of parenting: To make God known to our children. And to discover and explore who our children are through God's measure. To uncover the individual potential woven into each of our kids and to help cultivate that seed of purpose into full bloom.

Regardless of what your neighbors or the soccer team or Aunt Rose thinks.

NOT NORMAL

We put a high premium on "normal" in our culture. It's often one of those things we identify by what it is *not*. We say that a certain behavior is just "not normal." We say that it wasn't a "normal" day.

I'll own right up front that I've grown accustomed to the moniker "weird." Once you birth eight children and start driving a fifteen-passenger van, you've pretty much sealed up the adjective. Also, I live in Austin, Texas, which delights itself in stating "Keep Austin Weird."

We are not a "normal" family.

We have five girls and three boys—ranging in age from twenty-five to nine-year-old twins. We homeschool. I'm one of those weird long-distance runners.

We are not normal.

But we didn't start out that way. We didn't start out thinking we wanted eight children. Or seven. Or six. Or two.

Frankly, I thought I'd be fortunate if I could talk my husband into letting me have a kitten.

It wasn't that we didn't like kids. It's just that when we married, we had a well-laid plan for the first decade of our marriage. I would continue in my television and radio career while Michael finished his law degree. Once his law degree was complete, we would head to the East Coast—preferably New York City or Washington, D.C. By that point, I would have had enough air time to break into one of those competitive television markets, and Michael could get on with a big law firm and begin laying the groundwork to run for political office. Once those goals were achieved, we would take an extended vacation to Europe, where we would get pregnant—probably in Greece or Italy. Somewhere around the ten-year mark in the marriage.

So when we had a pregnancy test go all "two blue lines" on us seven months into our marriage while on a Utah ski vacation, we found ourselves firmly outside the norm of our young, achievement-oriented peer group. Far outside.

We weren't where we wanted to be financially or professionally. We were relatively young—some of the youngest expectant parents we knew among our colleagues and peers. We weren't following the normal timeline for an ambitious, goal-driven couple.

Yet somehow, even in our surprise, we knew we were embarking on a blessed route.

Our daughter Madison's birth three months after our first anniversary introduced us to the beauty of allowing "normal" to become undefined.

Seven years into our marriage, we had two precious little girls and a newborn baby boy. Most of our friends were now marrying and starting families of their own. We were finally back on what we saw as the normal path. We figured our family was complete. Three kids was a plenty big family for us, and we'd still be relatively young once these children were off to school. We could then reinstitute the original ten-year plan.

Except that the Lord had been teaching us the beauty of being "peculiar."

And we found that we had become less consumed with being seen as a "normal" family and more interested in being a family set apart for Him. And, eventually, a family comprised of eight children and two highly caffeinated parents.

It's amazing to see what the Lord will do when we're willing to step outside the confines of "normal."

And really, I'm not sure I would even be able to identify what a "normal" family looks like. The 2010 U.S. Census count of 1.83 as the "normal" number of children in a household is not a statistic that can hold in practicum.[1] Not that the number of children in a family is an indicator of normal, anyway. We had neighbors with two kids and a yellow Lab. And an adorable house. And a beautifully landscaped yard. Both of the parents had escaped from Iran as children back in the '70s. The husband's family made their way to England, the wife's to Germany. They each ultimately made their way to the US, where they met and married. That's not exactly a normal tale.

Behind every picket fence lies the most incredible story. Overwhelming challenge. Breaking heartache. Decided joy. Unusual choices. Unfamiliar beauty. Reconsidered success. Undefined normal. Discovered individuality.

You look around your neighborhood, your church, your school, gauging how your kid is doing based on what you assume is a correctly calibrated thermometer of achievement.

But there is only one true Measure.

And that Measure's definition of a successful life is far different from our society's.

Did you know that the word *normal* only appears in the Bible once in the New International Version? It doesn't appear at all in the King James. Or the English Standard. Only twice in the American Standard—and never in reference to God's expectations for His people. God doesn't say, "Go raise your children to be normal kids. Go be normal and average. Set a goal to be as homogenous as the culture around you, and use their definition as your guide."

At least, not in the Word I'm reading.

As a matter of fact, God seems to indicate He wants quite the opposite. He wants us to be downright peculiar. He wants us to be weird and to raise weird progeny.

As in, He actually says it. He wants us to be His peculiar kids. His not-normal children. His sons and daughters that are set apart, an unusual treasure.

It seems that our Father is all about raising originals. In fact, the Bible has five different places where God specifically, lovingly, adoringly calls His kids "weird."

Exodus 19:5 says, ". . . if ye will obey my voice indeed, and keep my covenant, then ye shall be a peculiar treasure unto me above all people . . ." (KJV).

The book of Deuteronomy twice declares God's people as His "peculiar people."

The book of Titus states, "Who gave himself for us, that he might redeem us from all iniquity, and purify unto himself a peculiar people, zealous of good works" (Titus 2:14 KJV).

And then there's my favorite, that gorgeous line from the apostle Peter: "But ye are a chosen generation, a royal priesthood, an holy nation, a peculiar people . . ." (1 Peter 2:9 KJV).

I know, I know. The King James language is a bit fanciful here. More modern translations render "peculiar" as "chosen."

But both the Hebrew and Greek terms in these five passages speak to a sense of being a treasure, something precious and rare, something different and unique in the eyes of God.

I'd rather be God's odd duck—a peculiar, original kid—than the world's poster child for normal. I'd rather be His uncommon possession than common in His interest. As for me and my house, weird sounds better and better. Particularly when it sounds like "treasured."

ONLY AN ILLUSION

It looks like such a magical place.

And I fall for it over and over.

At the immaculate granite counter stands a slender mother, her blond hair pulled into a sleek low ponytail. She fills a gleaming pasta pot from a white farmhouse sink's stylish gooseneck faucet. An attentive and obedient Jack Russell terrier stands alert by her feet, anxious for a stray treat. Two adorable, perfectly dressed and coiffed children sit at the expanse of the kitchen island, sharing crayons and paper as they draw and create and dream. A bundle of freshly washed carrots, their bright green tops still attached, lay in a colander, a vibrant pop of color in the creamy white kitchen. While mother and children are quietly enjoying the daily dinnertime prep, the father is most likely on his way home from a prosperous and fulfilling day at the office. A frosted white cake, mouthwateringly displayed on a vintage glass cake stand, will be served after those adorable children eat two full servings of fresh veggies. I'm sure light jazz is playing in the background. And the scent of a vanilla-lavender candle perfumes the air.

Perfection. What normal family life should look like on a weekday afternoon.

I'm a sucker for it—those scenes depicted in home decorating magazines. I know it's just magazine mythology. But I buy into it every time.

Somehow, in my head, I allow myself to believe that someone with a camera has snuck in, unprompted, like a modern-day anthropologist on field assignment, happening upon this tranquil scene. *This is what every home is like*, I think. *It's what mine should be like*, I scold myself. Surely, all across America, this scene of normalcy is being played out in pristine homes at this very moment.

And then I look up from the pages of the magazine and take in my own household decor.

Piles of laundry that have been sorted but have yet to be washed make haystacks down the hall from the front door. Someone has used the guest bathroom off the foyer as a personal dressing room, and every item of discarded clothing lies in repose in the order in which it was taken off, less-than-fresh underwear adorning the top of the pile. Broken crayons and food wrappers punctuate the baseboards like confetti, remnants of the ticker-tape parade of scooters and tricycles that have been ridden through the entry. Action figures and blocks are stacked precariously in the hall bookcases that house some of my dusty college textbooks. A pasta sauce handprint stands out like a crimson hieroglyph on the wall. And all of that is just within the first ten feet of my front door.

Total home decorating magazine fail.

I won't even try to impress you with the family room.

I know that the scenes illustrated in those magazines are carefully crafted. I know that the model depicting the mom probably doesn't even have kids and may have just graduated from high school last week. I know that a team of hair stylists smoothed and conditioned her casual ponytail into gleaming submission. I know those two kids probably aren't related and may have been picking their noses between camera frames. I know that someone made big bucks to come set those fresh carrots just so and spritz them with oil and water to make them shiny. And I know that the darling Jack Russell terrier is better known as a Jack Russell terror.

Yet somehow I've allowed these mythological images to creep into my psyche and become the definition of "normal." Somehow, those scenes become a backdrop of comparison for me, something I'm supposed to achieve in my home life without the benefit of stylists, stagers, and lighting experts.

And that's just a message I let creep in at only the cosmetic level. If I do exactly what the advertisers hope I will do, purchasing the products and expectations set in this scene supposedly will bring my children happiness and fulfillment and life direction.

It's pretty amazing what we allow to creep in on a deeper level.

We say that we want our kids to have "normal" childhoods. And by "normal," we mean privileged, easy, achievement-laden. Our magazine-spread ideal captures that vision. From a well-meaning place, we want to protect our kids from disappointment, lack, frustration, and hurt. But all the while—even in their earliest developmental stages—a truth is played out before us that takes the myth to task. Cutting teeth causes discomfort. Learning to crawl leads to rug burns. Trying to walk results in a few falls. It's right there in front of us, even if we don't want to see it. Growing up has its bumps and bruises. And that applies to the emotional stages of growth and development as well.

As Christian parents, we often say that we believe our children have special calls on their lives, unique assignments woven into the fiber of their beings, purposes they are to fulfill. But we don't want anyone to think they are weird. And we don't want them to skin their knees as they walk on the path laid out for them.

We have become a culture of parents who strive to create what we call "normal" childhoods for our kids, believing if we can achieve that magical ideal, we'll be rewarded with sparkling, popular, shiny kids. Our recipe is simple: one part idyllic childhood equals one part well-balanced, productive adult. If we can just live in the right house in the right neighborhood and keep our kids clothed in the latest fashions and ensure they make every team or squad they try out for—and if we can get them into the right college—then, surely, normal, successful people will be the result. Oh, and they'll be good Christians too. You know, after a little "normal" teenage rebellion and all.

The childhoods of the most significant personalities in the Bible, however, often strayed far from what we call "normal." Isaac led a nomadic life under the scorn of an older half-brother. Joseph spent his teenage years in servitude in Egypt—and then in prison. David became a giant killer and a ballad bringer for King Saul. Samuel spent his sixth birthday working alongside an aging priest. Esther missed prom but still managed to become queen. Mary had an out-of-wedlock pregnancy to explain. Jesus spent His days absorbing the poetic combination of theology and carpentry. Timothy navigated his teen years suspended between a worldly Greek father and a believing mother.

What's normal, anyway? We want our children to be seen as extraordinary, but we don't want them to have any extraordinary experiences other than that family trip to Disney World. Ironic, no?

LIFESTYLES OF THE MOABITES AND FAMOUS

As far as family trees go, this one gets a little thin near the top.

As in, no branches. For a rather unsavory reason.

There really isn't a pretty way to tell the tale.

It's a story that tends to not make it into children's Bible storybooks, which generally jump from Lot's wife becoming a pillar of salt straight to Abraham and Sarah welcoming Isaac into their family.

But it's in there.

After Lot and his daughters flee Sodom and Gomorrah, after Lot's wife looks back to see God's wrath poured out on those hedonistic hovels and turns into the original Morton Salt Girl, Lot and his daughters hightail it to the high country and take up residence in a cave. There, sequestered from civilization, with no internet dating and no cute guys in the cave next door, Lot's oldest daughter hatches a plan—a plan that sends a cringe throughout history.

She pulls her younger sister aside and says, "Our father is getting old and there's not a man left in the country by whom we can get pregnant. Let's get our father drunk with wine and lie with him. We'll get children through our father—it's our only chance to keep our family alive" (Genesis 19:31–32 MSG).

Both the older and the younger daughter get pregnant with baby boys as a result of this agenda. The oldest daughter names her son Moab, and the younger daughter names hers Ammon.

It plays out like some kind of Bible version of the 1947 Latham and Jaffe song, "I'm My Own Grandpa." Moab and Ammon are both the sons and grandsons of Lot. They are half-brothers and cousins. A tangle of genetics and sin, DNA and incest.

Bleh.

Not a terribly notable pedigree for a people.

Ultimately, the descendants of Moab became the Moabites, residing in the mountainous area on the eastern shore of the Dead Sea. The descendants of Ammon headed deeper into the deserts of Arabia.

The Moabites placed their focus on Chemosh, the deity of the region. And his consort, Astarte. And sometimes, for good measure, a little Baal worship was thrown in. Just to cover all the bases.

From the archaeological discovery of what is called the Chemosh

Stone, we learn that worship of Chemosh often involved human sacrifice, preferably by fire. And child sacrifice was common as an attempt to appease this temperamental and touchy idol. The Moabities left the monotheistic belief system of their forefather Lot and created a bloody, polytheistic stew from the cultures around them, embracing blood rituals and libation.

While the child sacrifices of the Moabites horrify us, they were normal in their world. They were an accepted part of their life. Theirs was a culture steeped in superstition and sacrifice.

Fast-forward 700 years into Moabite history and an interesting person shows up on the radar.

It was famine that took Elimelech and his wife, Naomi, into Moabite country with their two small sons. They'd left their hometown of Bethlehem and traveled over challenging terrain to arrive in the pagan country of the descendants of Lot. Jewish tradition says that Elimelech was a wealthy member of the Bethlehem community who was heartbroken about his inability to help all his starving community members. And so he left his homeland to escape the famine and his shame.

After he and Naomi arrive in Moab with their children, they settle there for a number of years. Elimelech passes away and their sons, Mahlon and Kilion, marry local girls. But tragedy strikes again when Mahlon and Kilion also die, and Naomi is left in a foreign land, her only family her daughters-in-law, Orpah and Ruth.

Cue the mother-in-law jokes.

Naomi decides this whole Moab thing hasn't worked out so well and plans to head back to Bethlehem. Initially, both Orpah and Ruth begin the trek with her. But after some miles and some discussion, Orpah makes a U-turn and heads back to the hills. Back to "normal."

Ruth, however, declares she'll leave her "normal" childhood behind and make her future with the one true God in the homeland of Naomi. She takes the conventions of Moab and exchanges them for loyalty to the woman who has become her spiritual mother. They continue to Bethlehem along a road known in ancient times as the King's Highway.

Literally.

And prophetically.

Because Ruth is on her way to becoming the ancestor of kings.

I love the lesson of Ruth's decision. She was raised in a culture that seems appalling to us. But it would have been normal for her. The myth of normalcy in her Moabite childhood centered around a highly marketed idol whose very name meant Destroyer. It was tradition.

We often parent based on the traditions we see around us. Some of our culture's accepted parenting practices, which overemphasize "fitting in" and the vague ideal of a folklorish "happiness," can destroy those traits in our kids that are singular and unique and uncommon. All because "normal" is more important. Sometimes, we sacrifice the hearts of who our children truly are in the interest of appeasing the judging voices around us.

Don't miss what the good townsfolk of Bethlehem say about Ruth all throughout the book of the Bible that bears her name. Mostly, she's called "Ruth the Moabite," lest anyone forget her skinny family tree. The first time her future husband, Boaz, lays eyes on her and asks who she is, he's told, "She is the Moabite who came back from Moab with Naomi. She said, 'Please let me glean and gather among the sheaves behind the harvesters'" (Ruth 2:6–7). They weren't just talking about the geography of Ruth's background. They were referring to her unsavory heritage of paganism and incest.

But Ruth exchanged Moabite norms for eternal truths— truths about loyalty and love and service. About being set apart. About purpose.

When Ruth makes that decision on the road known as the
King's Highway—the decision to walk away from the Moabite
myth of normal—she not only impacts her own life but also paves
the way for her descendants. She marries Boaz and gives birth
to a son. She becomes the matriarch of incredible descendants.
Descendants who include King David. And Jesus Christ.

I've seen modern-day folks putting their kids' hearts on the
altar of Chemosh. There's no visible fire, no bloodletting. But you
still see it. The kid who is miserable on the baseball field and the
father who won't accept that this boy is no Nolan Ryan. The child
driven to the limits of time and effort for academic achievement,
with no room to dream. The girl pushed to look a certain way and
act a certain way, all out of a mother's desire for attention.

The Moabite parents of Ruth's childhood weren't acting out
of the norm of their culture; they were acting exactly in the center
of that norm, buying into the myth. We need to be checking the
corners of our parenting motives, sweeping out the cobwebs of
motherly mythology and fatherly fables that place more value on
societal and—dare I say it—church opinion than on embracing
the biblical blessing of taking the King's Highway that leads to
peculiar purpose.

When I look at the magazine spread of my parenting expectations and my idealism, I'm sometimes startled to see what I've
placed there. While it's appropriate to protect our kids from
serious trauma, we must allow them to feel the ache of cutting
teeth, the sting of skinned knees, the bruises that come with
learning to walk. They need to see the homeless, the outcasts, the
lost. Compassion and character can't be taught from a textbook.
We whisper, we shield, we use euphemisms for the unsavory,
the difficult, the upsetting events all around us, in an effort to
maintain this illusion of normalcy. Is it any wonder we see kids
shell-shocked and wavering in their faith when they discover, at

the cusp of adulthood, that even grown-ups make mistakes and disappoint? If we have curved every grade and cushioned every effort, should we be surprised that they don't know how to grab hold of their dreams and press through setbacks on the way to their God-ordained futures? We are sacrificing important, shaping experiences to appease an ever-hungry idol named Normal.

As we seek the contours of the parenting journey, we must assess how much "normal" we're unconsciously pressing toward. "Normal" is so subtle it can be hard to spot when it has fixed itself as a filter of our perception. Be on the lookout for these areas as you declutter your parenting closet to make room for the exceptional:

- As a child, you felt the sting of peer rejection, and you want to inoculate your kid against it.
- You come from a background that has some odd twists, turns, and dramas, and you long for stability, which you may mislabel as "normal." Stability and normalcy can be two different things.
- You like the predictable, the routine. Anything outside of "normal" is scary for you.
- You dread standing out in a crowd. You're content to be a beige wallflower, happy to let others be the trendsetters and the pioneers.
- You were raised in a setting where decorum and etiquette trumped individuality and creativity.
- You love God, but you've seen people be "weird" for Him . . . and it got truly weird, indeed. That's not a place you want to go.
- You've bought into the idea that "normal" is a place where discomforts are few, embarrassing moments are mitigated, and edges are buffered. Normal feels safe.

When I look at the life of Zélie the lacemaker, and when I read her writings and look at the lessons of her craft and her parenting, I discover a beautiful truth. Zélie was well known and sought out for her Alençon lace, a highly desired and cherished design. Though it looks delicate, Alençon lace is one of the strongest laces produced. Its edge is woven with thicker thread, which then allows for the "field" of the lace—that place where you can see the design and whimsy and originality—to be displayed. That strong border, in combination with the creativity of the weaving within the border, makes for durable, exquisite expressions of thread. Zélie's skill in creating that kind of lace played out in her parenting. Her daughters were raised within strong borders of faith, family, compassion, and integrity, while their individual threads were allowed to find original expression within the fields of that border.

Alençon lace is a powerful image of the gorgeous word "original." Yes, original means those things that are completely unique, completely new, completely individual. But original also means the initial template—the origin—from which everything else takes its form. In being more focused on raising originals than on trying to achieve the world's "normal," we take the original template of God's righteousness and wisdom, and allow the original threads of our kids to play within those borders, yielding a weave of life completely unique and completely grounded.

As we begin to discern the purpose of our parenting and the individuality of our kids, let's make sure we are seeking first the edge of God's desire over the uniform normality of the world's definition. Let's embrace His guidance and revel in the wide field of grace in which we weave, we parent, we pray. We can do better than normal. We can weave toward original.

PART 2

THE TIES THAT TANGLE

Avoiding Parenting Pitfalls

CHAPTER 3

IT'S NOT JUST ABOUT FINDING THEM THAT JOB

*It takes courage to grow up and
become who you really are.*
E. E. Cummings

I ONCE HEARD a story about a mom whose young daughter was driving her crazy demanding a turtle. To tell passing turtle fancy from true turtle commitment, mom told daughter she'd consider getting her a turtle if the daughter was willing to do the necessary research to validate her turtle-ownership need.

Smart mom.

One of my kids sort of once mentioned wanting a puppy. I said okay. Ten years later, we have ten-year-old miniature long-hair dachshund/Pomeranian mix dogs that, when they aren't busy shedding said long hair and yipping ad infinitum, are happily peeing and piddling everywhere but the yard. And these dogs have somehow become "mine."

Lesson learned.

Back to the smart mom. She required this turtle research workup and, to her surprise, the daughter enthusiastically jumped in. The girl went to the library and looked up types of turtles and turtle habitats and determined the cost of keeping a turtle. She made a little report and handed it in to her mom, complete with turtle drawings.

The mom had figured the required research would temper the turtle embers. But no. So she added another layer.

The daughter would be required to raise the funds necessary to acquire the desired turtle and to supply all its turtle needs.

Given this new challenge, the daughter swung into action. She negotiated payment for performing extra chores and assessed her financial situation.

To the mom's surprise, her daughter raised the money. The turtle obsession remained.

All hurdles having been cleared by the diligent daughter, the two went to the pet store, turtle money burning a hole in the daughter's Hello Kitty wallet. They selected turtle food and nutritional supplements and chose various habitat items, even adding a few decor pieces to accessorize.

And then they arrived at the glass enclosure, the place where the newest member of the family was currently nestled with his turtle brothers and sisters. Candidates were considered, pros and cons discussed. After a decision was reached, a pet store employee gently removed The One from the glass enclosure and handed the turtle to the mom. Caught up with pride for her daughter's determination and perseverance, the mom extended the turtle toward her daughter's deserving hands. The moment was perfect.

Except . . .

Upon feeling the clammy, scaly reality of the turtle, the daughter shrieked and dropped the coveted turtle onto the tile floor. "Mom! I said I wanted to *have* a turtle! I didn't say I wanted to *hold* a turtle!"

WHEN YOU GROW UP . . .

As it turns out, there's a big difference between having a turtle and holding a turtle. And in that difference between the having and the holding is found the first tangle we'll want to look out for in the raising of our originals.

As we go about this business of raising up the next generation, there are tangles we need to watch out for if we want to protect what is original and singular in our kids. These seemingly innocuous tangles are so embedded in our culture that we might miss them. But their entrapping components can stunt our broader vision, just like a band placed around the tender trunk of a young tree can choke it from future growth if it becomes too tight.

We introduce the first tangle when our kids are young. *What do you want to be when you grow up?* we ask them. I suppose we're practicing for the adult equivalent, *So what do you do?* We're a culture that tends to base our identities on the jobs we have. We're programmed to believe a certain career can bring us joy and fulfillment. We daydream about the wealth and prestige the perfect job will bring. And we pass this mentality on to our kids.

While we want our kids to reach higher and achieve more, it's not always about them. Sometimes it's about us. Truth be told, we have a little of our own identity wrapped up in our children's achievements.

There's a unique turn of phrase amongst my relatives in the Deep South. They'll say that Cousin Mark "made a doctor" or Cousin Suzie "made a lawyer." What they mean is that Cousin Mark studied medicine and became a physician and that Cousin Suzie went to law school, passed the bar, and opened an office. But I think there's also an embedded meaning to the phrase. Cousin Mark may have "made a doctor," but being a doctor made *him*.

He's going to know financial security and prestige. Cousin Suzie will be respected as an attorney. She'll be like those lawyers on television—beautifully dressed and stressed and important. Yes, they may have "made" doctor and lawyer, but doctor and lawyer will make *them*—make their futures, make their worth.

That's a lot of pressure to put on a profession.

IN THE CENTER OF YOUR CALLING

What do the following words have in common?

Record store clerk. Singer. Childcare provider. Blogger. House sitter. Public speaker. Hardware store specialist. Shoe store salesperson. Nursery school teacher. Vocalist for jingles. Radio show host. Ministry leader. Business and marketing consultant. Teacher. Video editor. Writer. Medical file organizer. Photographer. Television reporter. Labor coach. Event planner. Voice-over artist. Wedding planner.

Do you see any thread of connection, other than job titles?

Well, there's one—those are some of the jobs I've had. They're not cute rewrites of my experiences as a mom, though I've applied many of the things I've learned in those jobs in my mom career. They're actual professions I've had. And my experience is not that unusual. *Forbes* magazine reported that the average person today will hold about 15–20 jobs over the course of a lifetime. That's a far cry from the era of starting your first job with the same company you retire from.

I have a friend who used to be a chiropractor and is now a marketing consultant. Another friend, formerly a lawyer, is now a broker for fine wines. My pastor, Randy Phillips, started out as an office supply salesman, then moved into a successful music career with the contemporary Christian group Phillips, Craig and Dean, before becoming a senior pastor. And yet another friend enjoyed great success in professional sales until he transitioned into a writing career. It's not that unusual.

And yet . . .

I continue to encounter many parents who are terribly concerned about their children's future careers. They want their child to find *the* job, *the* career path, *the* vocation. They're still buying into the myth that the right career will protect their kid from uncertainty and hard times. That it will *make* them.

But let's invert the box a bit.

I think we jump onto the what-do-you-want-to-be bandwagon because we're searching for threads of identity within our children. If we can just learn what they aspire to, then we'll see what they're made of, what skills and talents and dreams they have. We think that what they want to *be* will help us understand who they *are*.

Understandable. But flawed.

This next statement isn't going to sound very live-your-dreams friendly. But it can be very freeing.

The thing that makes your heart sing, that gives you purpose, that place where you know you're right in the center of your calling—it may never be what you do as a paid vocation. It may never be your official "job." And yet you can still do it. You can still allow your heart to sing. You can still walk in your purpose while making a living at your desk job. And you haven't missed God, and He hasn't missed you.

Evidence shows us the odds are pretty low that a certain job will bring us automatic fulfillment and purpose and vision. But we still spout the gospel of corporate drive instead of the gospel of *God* being the source of fulfillment and purpose and vision.

While work is important and necessary, we can't saddle it with more than it was meant to provide. I've had jobs in which I've found amazing fulfillment. I've also had jobs in which I've found amazing frustration. But God tells me to do all work—the fulfilling and the frustrating—as if unto Him.

We can hamstring our kids and ourselves if we think a job is beneath us. Some of those entry-level jobs can be the very things that ultimately open the door to our destiny. As Colossians 3:23–24 says, "Whatever you do, work at it with all your heart, as working for the Lord, not for human masters, since you know that you will receive an inheritance from the Lord as a reward. It is the Lord Christ you are serving."

When we become trapped in the tangle of vocation, we can pass on a message of fear to our kids. We can set them up to believe they have no voice in working with a tyrant or putting up with poor practices, all because we've so heavily emphasized how important it is to have a "good" job. Yes, there are times when God allows us to stay in a difficult work situation in order to strengthen and grow and teach us. But I've also seen Christians remain in horrid situations out of fear, trusting in their dismal job more than they trust in God's loving provision.

SWOONING APPRENTICE

Our oldest daughter, Madison, a graduate of the University of Texas, had big plans to go into research and medicine. She and her baby sister, Merci, are very close, their seventeen-year age difference giving them a special blend of sibling connection as Madison has been like a favorite aunt to Merci, loving her and spoiling her and taking her out for frozen yogurt and doing her nails. Madison and Merci are also close due to the stroke Merci experienced at birth that resulted in left-side hemiplegia, or weakness on the left side. It's also called cerebral palsy. All of our kids have been involved in the process of helping Merci with the physical therapy exercises designed to help her gain better use of her left side and loosen her cramped muscles, and Madison—being the oldest—has spent a lot of time helping her baby sister.

For a while, Merci was receiving regular onobotulinumtoxin A (Botox) injections. Now, don't go judging me and thinking I'm some kind of out-of-control baby beauty pageant mom. The Botox was administered in Merci's left arm and leg to try to loosen up muscles that were staying permanently flexed due to the stroke. (Okay, I'll admit that I did ask jokingly-not-jokingly on a few occasions if Merci's neurologist might share a little of that Botox with Merci's mama and treat Mama's crumpled forehead. The neurologist declined.) Because the injections had to be placed fairly deep within her muscles, Merci had to undergo general anesthesia each time she went in for treatment. The procedure itself was quick and, because of the anesthesia, painless.

As part of Madison's UT coursework for completing her degree in neurobiology, we made arrangements for her to observe one of Merci's Botox procedures. Madison had been watching surgical procedures via video and was excited to see firsthand how the neurologist would use electrodes on Merci's arm and leg to determine where to place the injections and how that would correspond for Merci on a sensorineural level. The neurologist was supportive of having big sister pre-med student Madison along for the ride, and there had even been talk of a summer internship.

We arrived at the hospital early, went through the usual pre-op procedures, and let Merci select what "flavor" of anesthesia she wanted for the day's events as Madison took notes. Finally, it was time to take Merci back to the surgical suite. Because Merci and I were regulars at this point, I was allowed to walk back to the procedure room with both girls and put Merci up on the table, staying with her until she drifted off to sleep. Giving Madison a quick hug, I told her how excited I was for her to have this opportunity. Then I headed out to the waiting room, equipped with books and tablet to keep my mind occupied. No matter how many times we'd been through this, I was always churning a bit inside.

I grabbed some coffee and got situated with my reading materials. The procedure usually took about an hour. While the injections didn't take long, it did take a little while to make sure Merci was comfortably under and then came out of the anesthesia well.

I was just pages into my book when a nurse showed up in the waiting room, calling my name. My heart pounding wildly, I calculated they'd only been back there about ten minutes. I stood up, books and reading glasses scattering, heart in my throat. "What's wrong? Why are they done so soon?"

The nurse placed her hand on my arm reassuringly. "Everything's fine. Your daughter just had a little spell, but she's fine."

My mind raced. What kind of "spell"? Merci had never had a "spell" under anesthesia. But before I could ask anything else, another nurse led my daughter out to the waiting room.

Not Merci.

Madison.

The pre-med student with the aspiration of making doctor.

Madison.

Green to the gills where she wasn't white as a sheet.

Oh—*that* daughter.

Things had gotten underway as usual. The anesthesiologist had made sure Merci was comfortably out. The neurologist had come in and graciously introduced Madison to the team. She'd called Madison over to watch where she was marking injection sites and using an electrode device to find muscle tone. She'd filled the syringe and had begun to inject the first site on Merci's little leg.

And then Madison had felt the need to back up.

And back up some more.

And back up all the way to the tiled wall of the surgical suite.

And then Madison had slid down the tiled wall of the surgical suite.

And then slumped over.

At which point she was competing against her baby sister for medical attention.

At which point a couple of nurses brought her to me.

Madison was embarrassed as she could possibly be. And shocked. She had watched multiple surgical procedures online. She'd dreamed of working with patients, stitching wounds, doing exploratory surgeries. She had committed incredible amounts of time to her studies and was one of the top students in her class. She was preparing for the MCAT, for heaven's sake.

But . . .

As it turned out, she wanted to *have* a turtle, not *hold* a turtle.

It's hard to know what you want to do when you haven't had the opportunity to do it. Our modern culture seems to have lost the art of apprenticeship. We've gotten so busy trying to get our kids into the best schools and encouraging them to major in something that will bring them vocational and financial success that we often skip the step of seeing if our child really *knows* what it will be like. We don't bother to find out if they figuratively (and literally, in Madison's case) have the stomach for it.

I recently spoke at an event organized by a friend of mine, who teaches a unique high school course that matches students with mentors. A student considering the architecture field spends a semester shadowing a professional architect. A student wondering about a career in real estate tracks a Realtor. A student thinking about being a veterinarian spends the shadow semester with a vet. And they don't just visit the mentor once or even a couple times. These students are with their mentors many, many times throughout the semester, experiencing multiple facets of their respective vocations.

My friend had asked me to be the keynote speaker for the year-end banquet celebrating this student-mentor experience. But before I took the podium, several students spoke. Some had discovered that their personalities, temperaments, and interests really were a good match for the career they'd been considering. But one girl found that the career she'd idolized, the professional path she'd hinged her college plans upon, was not a good fit. At all. In discovering this, she'd looked more deeply into who she was and why she wished to pursue this career path.

Sometimes one of the most valuable steps to learning who you are is learning who you *aren't*.

A child who loves all kinds of little creatures, rescues lost puppies, and names every roly-poly in the flowerbed may ultimately become a vet. But what that child is really showing is a gift for compassion. A gift for nurturing. He is "others-focused" and protective. That's the gem. That's the thread we seek. That beautiful strand, carefully discovered and lovingly curated, will serve him well at the deepest core of his life, regardless of where his work takes him.

> SOMETIMES ONE OF THE MOST VALUABLE STEPS TO LEARNING WHO YOU ARE IS LEARNING WHO YOU *AREN'T*.

It's fascinating to look at the vocations of people in the Bible, individuals whom the Word records as having a specific purpose in God's plan. When the prophet Samuel shows up at Jesse's ranch, ready to anoint someone as king, he doesn't tell Jesse he's out recruiting the next king of Israel. When the Lord initially tells Samuel to go to Jesse's place to find the future king, Samuel tells the Lord he's worried that word will get back to Saul, the reigning king. And if that were to happen, there would be heck to pay. So the Lord instructs Samuel to simply say he's there to consecrate Jesse and his boys and to make a sacrifice to the Lord. No mention of anointed vocation necessary.

As Jesse's sons arrive for the event, Samuel watches them closely. First he sees Eliab—handsome, tall, strong—and thinks, *This has got to be the guy.* But the Lord tells Samuel, "Do not consider his appearance or his height, for I have rejected him. The LORD does not look at the things people look at. People look at the outward appearance, but the LORD looks at the heart" (1 Samuel 16:7).

And so the pageant continues, as one by one Jesse's sons walk in front of Samuel, with Samuel realizing one by one that each was *not* the one. It seems that all the options have been exhausted.

Then Jesse remembers that he has one more kid—the youngest, David, who's out taking care of sheep somewhere in the back forty. When David is brought into Samuel's presence, the Lord tells Samuel that David *is* the one. And so Samuel anoints David in front of his brothers.

But notice what's missing. Samuel never says David is being anointed as the next *king*. A job title is never mentioned. Maybe Jesse had an inkling of what might be up, but Samuel is on a secret mission. What *does* result from this anointing is the Spirit of the Lord comes on David, and not just "kind of." The Word records that the Spirit comes in power.

Over the coming years, David will wear many vocational titles. *Shepherd. Rock slinger. Musician. Armor bearer. Mercenary. Career army.*

And, finally, *king.*

The unique threads God had placed in David allowed him to become the anointed king. But the same anointed David carried the power of God with him through shepherding, Philistine-felling, performing as a one-boy pop band in Saul's court. The personality of his heart, his passion, his integrity, his courage were with him through it all, regardless of if he was singing to God in a pasture or in the palace.

The vocation didn't make the man.

The man made the vocation.

Moses worked for his father-in-law. Rahab was employed as the original Working Girl. Ezra tasted food for the king's kitchen. Paul sewed tents. Luke had a medical practice. Matthew collected taxes. Peter fished for a living. Phoebe designed textiles. And yet we don't remember them for how they made a living. We remember them for how they lived.

I would love for my kids to find vocations in which they blossom. If their beautiful threads translate into glowing careers, fantastic! But, more importantly, I hope their beautiful threads shine even if the job isn't awesome or the benefits are nonexistent.

Madison, my fainting pre-med major, finished her degrees in French and neurobiology. To date, she's not headed to med school so she can put MD after her name and "make" a doctor. She's taken her ability to focus deeply, her attention to detail, and her adoration of little ones to create a career for herself matching childcare givers to children. She uses her beautiful threads to recruit, train, and manage loving, nurturing caregivers while ensuring that the kids receive the best care possible.

She may go on to have several other careers. Careers in which her threads will shine brightly.

The vocation isn't making the woman.

The woman is making the vocation.

REAL SUCCESS

What if we *really* set our kids up for success?

What if we were honest with them that sometimes the American dream of career isn't always fun?

What if we let them know that sometimes bosses are mean and coworkers are difficult and work can be just . . . boring?

What if we let them know that their career doesn't give them their sense of identity?

It may not sound terribly American, but boy, is it biblical. Joseph had to deal with an employer's cougar wife and a vengeful boss. Daniel and his friends were snatched from home, most likely castrated, and put to work in the enemy's palace. No chance to take career compatibility quizzes.

What if we knew our kids' temperaments, their one-of-a-kind threads, so well that we could help equip them for whatever challenges they might encounter in the working world?

What if we could say to them, "You know, with your curious thread of being people-oriented and caring so much about what others think, let's talk about setting boundaries. You'll need to know how to keep a good work/personal life balance."

What if we could help our goal-centered kid learn to compete and compete well, but not at the expense of his integrity or at the expense of others?

We need to set our kids up for success, no matter how capricious the currents of career change.

Some of our dearest friends are the parents of seven children. Three of their kids, at a very young age, formed a band that became an international sensation. These boys experienced a meteoric rise in popularity, giving concerts in sold-out arenas across the globe. Incredibly gifted, they played a variety of instruments and composed their own music. From a vocational standpoint, one might assume their careers were made, all at the tender ages of fifteen, thirteen, and ten. But their wise mom and dad—mentor parents to Michael and me—knew the music industry could be a fickle taskmaster.

While it was a joy to see the boys play big shows, our greatest privilege was seeing them in action at home. They washed dishes. They babysat their younger siblings. They did their chores. One day, at the height of the band's popularity, one of the boys spent a long time playing in the sandbox with my toddler son Justus. I watched as this young pop sensation tenderly brushed the sand from Justus's chubby little feet before putting his shoes back on. Another time, one of the boys insisted on holding my baby so I could go swimming—a welcome break for a tired mom. Even though the boys could have become defined by their musical success, their parents continued to curate the beautiful, curious threads in each of their children. Threads of compassion. Threads of playfulness. Threads of focus. Threads of diligence. Threads of joy. Threads of humility. And they didn't just do that for their three kids who were literal superstars. They've done it for their four other kids, who have watched their brothers from the wings.

The guys are still making music today. They're raising their own families. It's our joy to call them precious friends. But even if their music careers had come to a halt—even if they'd exited the stage and gone on to find "normal" jobs—I have no doubt that they would still carry the same character and their threads would still shine just as brightly. Their success is not that they've continued to make music. It's that they are generous, mature, caring, curious individuals. Their different personalities shine as they raise their kids and love their wives and build a legacy. It would have been easy for them to believe their music "made" them, but the thread seekers in their lives taught them the true heartbeat of the music is an orchestra of purpose, a life of compassion and generosity.

Let's always be on the lookout for the tangle of vocation. If our children find work that dovetails with their curious threads, praise God. But may we never tangle those threads with the ensnaring message that a job is what makes or breaks them. May we infuse and curate character into them so that, no matter how prestigious or plain the job is, the sheen of God's power shines in their lives and personalities and souls.

Just a vague awareness isn't enough to avoid the tangle of vocation. We need to be on the lookout that we might be communicating—be it intentionally or unintentionally—that career is the core of success.

ARE YOU TRAPPED?

If you were raised in a home where great value was placed on profession or title, you might be trapped in the tangle of vocation.

Just like families have certain holiday traditions or vacation spots or favorite meals, so too can families have a certain bent toward jobs. A family of doctors can place a high value on the next generation heading to medical school. A family line of builders or teachers or pastors can set the professional bar high. If our kids see us esteem more highly those who have careers the world labels "important," we're unintentionally telling them certain careers will make them more important. And that's in direct opposition to what the Bible says: "My dear friends, don't let public opinion influence how you live out our glorious, Christ-originated faith. If a man enters your church wearing an expensive suit, and a street person wearing rags comes in right after him, and you say to the man in the suit, 'Sit here, sir; this is the best seat in the house!' and either ignore the street person or say, 'Better sit here in the back row,' haven't you segregated God's children and proved that you are judges who can't be trusted?" (James 2:1–4 MSG).

If you come from a family background that envied the professional achievements of others, you might be trapped in the tangle of vocation.

Families who have struggled to make ends meet sometimes hold up the perceived ease and prestige of certain jobs as the embodiment of freedom, success, and achievement. Some of the most driven people I know come from a background in which they've felt the need to rise above their humble beginnings and prove that they've arrived. By pinning their identity on the perfect job, they hope to compensate for what they think they've missed out on both economically and socially. But that doesn't guarantee lasting joy.

If you love your work and have found identity and fulfillment through your career, you might be headed for the tangle of vocation.

For some of us, vocation and calling have collided with divine serendipity. We love our job, we live our job, we *are* our job. If that describes you, be aware that you might be giving your kids the message that's what all work should be—a congenial love affair between interests, identity, and economics. While I do pray that my kids love their work, I also need to let them know that there may be seasons—and some of them extended seasons— when work is not all that fulfilling.

For several years, my job was putting sequential stickers on medical files. Night after night, I placed sticker after sticker on file folders—crates and crates of file folders. It wasn't particularly inspiring, but it served an important purpose, as Michael and I focused on building his business while allowing me to work from home and be with our children. My older kids remember this season along with the years that Michael threw a paper route to supplement the income from his full-time job. And we are intentional to let our younger kids know that the work Michael and I now have—as much as we love it and as thankful as we are for it—didn't just happen. It began back in the days of stickers on medical files and second-job paper routes. And God honored it all.

What if, for some reason, God calls you out of your current profession? What if you were no longer able to fulfill the duties of your position? Do you know who you are apart from your career? Have you done the internal work of figuring it out?

If you have significant doubts or have experienced serious failure in the career choices you've made for yourself, you might be trapped in the tangle of vocation.

Maybe you're determined not to see your kids saddled with the same mistakes you've made. Maybe you're benevolently but autocratically trying to steer their aspirations. While you might have great wisdom to share from your failed career path, there's also great value in learning things firsthand for yourself. And then there's the importance of being flexible. Companies that used to offer their employees lifetime loyalty now experience buyouts and outsourcing. Plain and simple, the workplace has changed. You'll never be able to mitigate all the career challenges that could come your child's way, no matter the cautionary tale you have to tell.

It's estimated that over the course of a typical lifetime with a traditional work schedule, we will spend over 90,000 hours working. *Ninety thousand.* That's 5,400,000 minutes. Or 324,000,000 seconds.(Yes, I did the math—admittedly with a calculator.) It's a massive percentage of our lives, of our kids' lives. While I want my kids to be prepared to do a job, more importantly, I want them to be prepared to live those 90,000 hours with joy, character, compassion, and purpose, regardless of the task, the health care plan, the boss, or the retirement package. If I telegraph to the next generation that joy, character, compassion, and purpose are found *in* a career, rather than being things we bring *to* a career, I slip a noose on the pathway to adulthood—a noose that can clutch at the ankle and trip an eager heart.

So let's clear the trail of false expectations and misplaced personal worth. Whether in the stockroom or the boardroom, let our anthem to our children be this: We make the job. The job doesn't make us. And let's truly live this verse: "May the favor of the Lord our God rest on us; establish the work of our hands for us—yes, establish the work of our hands" (Psalm 90:17).

CHAPTER 4

IT'S NOT JUST ABOUT GETTING THEM THAT DEGREE

*Educating the mind without educating
the heart is no education at all.*

Aristotle

CENTRAL MISSISSIPPI.

1940.

Log cabin built under a big oak tree.

Dirt floor.

That's where my father was born—born to good, decent sharecroppers doing their best to coax butter beans and tomatoes from the mercurial Mississippi red clay.

From his rural beginnings, my dad went on to become a rocket scientist.

Literally.

If you were to have asked him how one makes a quantum leap like that, his answer would have been immediate and sure.

Education.

Early on, I learned that education was the ticket to achievement.

It had been my dad's way out of a humble beginning to trafficking in the cosmos. When you have that kind of a dad, any excuse you come up with for poor grades is never good enough. It's a new take on the classic, "I walked to school two miles in the snow uphill . . . both ways" adage. My dad could always up any conversation about education with his story of growing up on a tiny plot of farmland with only a few pairs of overalls to his name.

My dad's parents were sweet, hardworking, decent people. They adored their two boys, were committed to their church, and shared whatever they could grow with their neighbors. When crops failed, they headed to the Gulf Coast so that my grandfather could work in the shipyards. My dad's father died at the age of sixty-four, his lungs scarred from the emphysema he developed smearing asbestos on the inner lining of ships and his back permanently hunched from a lifetime of hard physical labor.

It was my dad's older brother, Bill, who first saw the potential of obtaining an education beyond the small country school he and my dad attended. Uncle Bill figured out a way to finance a college education for himself by signing up for the Army. In doing so, he cracked open the door to a wider world for my father. Bill became the first of the family to attend college, and when my dad graduated from high school, he followed suit. My dad's high school grades were not meritorious, his preparation for college not stellar, and his financial backing nonexistent. Nevertheless, the vision took hold and the fire ignited.

During summer breaks from college, my dad returned to the small town on the Gulf Coast where his parents were now living. Like his father, he did backbreaking work in the shipyards. Summer earnings saved, he'd head back to the university in the fall, where he would subsist on cheese sandwiches and carefully rotate his wardrobe of two shirts and one sweater.

He studied. And he studied some more. The door that his

older brother had shouldered open gave my dad a glimpse of something beyond his rural upbringing and hardscrabble labor. He spotted possibility's perimeter, a sliver of the place where his curious mind and inventive streak just might find resonance. The completion of one degree led to higher degrees and specialization.

Yes, my father's academic achievements opened doors to the heavens and the stars. It afforded him impressive letters after his name and provided well fiscally for our family. But as remarkable as all that is, it doesn't tell you anything about my dad's character. It doesn't tell you if he lived a fulfilling life or a fractured one. It doesn't tell you if he performed his work with integrity or if he used nefarious methods to secure contracts with NASA. It doesn't tell you if he fulfilled the purpose and call on his life.

And it certainly doesn't tell you anything about his relationship with God.

Lest you think I'm belittling the place and importance of education for our children, that I'm being disparaging about the minds and possibilities that learning can open, please know that I'm a huge advocate of the blessing of an education. In fact, it's also part of my spiritual history. One of the great, grand gifts of the Reformation was a drive toward literacy for all societal ranks so that people could read the Bible for themselves. That shift alone has had a massive impact on literacy rates as well as faith in general. I have dear friends who work in the field of education whom I respect and honor deeply. They are devoted to their profession, to their students, to the culture of learning. I couldn't be more proud of them, couldn't be more thankful.

And they are fighting an uphill battle. The statistics regarding our country's educational system hit hard. There's an expectation that teachers, besides actually teaching the curriculum, will be the primary source of character formation, moral advancement, and destiny development for their students—and that's despite dismal budgets, lack of parental involvement, and crowded classrooms. No wonder teachers are leaving the classroom in unprecedented numbers and finding other jobs. They simply can't meet the unrealistic expectations heaped upon them.

We've arrived at a place where we've loaded so many nonacademic expectations on our school systems. We've also come to a place where we believe that academics will provide all the purpose and navigation we need for life's journey. And we're placing those towering expectations on an overwhelmed and underfunded system that was never intended to provide character formation and moral direction for its students.

Make no mistake, education is important. It's also expanding. And equipping. Secular parenting philosophy would have us believe it's about the most important thing we can do for our kids. It certainly helped transform the trajectory of my own family of origin, taking my dad from a sharecropper's beginnings to developing engines and systems that put people on the moon. My in-laws spent their careers as elementary school teachers and principals, both of them exactly the kind of loving, conscientious people you would want to guide your child's education.

However . . .

Education is a tool. Yes, it is powerful. But its primary function is not to reveal destiny or individual sparkle. When we place the unfair expectation upon our educational system to provide our kids with spiritual wisdom and life mission, we oversell what education can do and undersell our responsibility as believing parents.

We've got some rewiring to do. Here in the US, we spend more money per student than any other country in the world while reaping less than impressive results. We've placed a huge premium on what we think education can do. We wring our hands that our students are being outperformed in science by students in South

Korea. We fret that German kids have higher math scores. But when we take a deeper look, we see that South Korean students have some of the highest suicide rates in the world.[2] Even here in the US, some of our most prestigious universities—like MIT—also have high suicide rates.[3] We've got some serious rethinking to do when it comes to evaluating success based on scholastic measures alone. Are we willing to sacrifice quality of life—even length of life—for higher test scores? To me, that feels like sacrificing our kids on the altar of the idol Chemosh.

It's easy to fall into the trap of placing more faith in SAT scores and Ivy League pedigrees than in the God who knit us together.

I get it. I come from a home that sent a strong message about education, and then I married into a family of educators. So it's no surprise I was determined to procure the finest education I could find for my kids. No sacrifice would be too great, no inconvenience too overwhelming.

I could have shipwrecked Michael and myself financially on the rocks of obtaining a premier Christian education for our oldest daughter, Madison. In a season where Michael was building a new business and our budget was being held together with duct tape and popsicle sticks, an unexpected tax refund convinced me that this was God's way of providing Madison an education at the top Christian school in our community. I pushed and harangued and pled with Michael for us to use the unexpected refund as tuition for this exemplary school. I argued that her academic career was critical, that her future hinged on being educated at the best school, that we needed to be willing to make whatever sacrifices necessary to ensure scholastic success. And so we headed for the administrative office, checkbook in hand, paperwork regarding Madison's intelligence and aptitude carefully filled out.

After rigorous testing and an interview process, Madison was accepted. I was ecstatic. And so Madison began her gold-plated, upper-crust education, uniforms and educational theory in abundance. She became an elite student.

Grade Pre-K.

Yep.

Pre-K.

People, please.

Pre-K.

Did she have a fun year? Yes! Was the school a sweet place, with caring teachers and a positive learning environment? Absolutely!

Was it worth the financial craziness that resulted from putting that many of our scarce dollars toward a top-shelf scholastic experience?

Um . . . no.

It's not that private education or public education or home-schools or charter schools are superior or inferior or neutral. It's that I had put far more trust and investment in a select Pre-K program than I did in God's ability to use whatever educational model worked best for our family situation and budget.

My misplaced trust made financial chaos of our year as we scrambled to cover basic bills while dropping off Madison twice a week in a carpool line that boasted vehicles costing more than our house. And when the year came to an end, I hadn't learned any more about Madison—about her curious threads—than when we'd started, other than the fact that she tended not to eat the sandwiches I packed for her school lunch if I put mustard on them. For as much money as we paid and as nice as the school was, they weren't all that interested in finding out what made Madison tick, what made her an original. Understandably, they were more concerned with maintaining the impressive testing scores and academic record of their total student population. Group dynamics, if you will.

Here's some shockingly good news: God is not limited or

empowered by your kid's mediocre or sparkling academic record. God can absolutely use someone who is a poor speller. It's not a moral failure if your kid isn't great at math. Educational success is not the same thing as spiritual success.

When we think about education and its role in equipping our kids for their futures, we need to be clear about what education can and cannot do. And we also need to be clear about what it *should* do.

Math and science aren't about math and science. They're about logic and critical thinking skills. That's missing from our national understanding about education, which seems to be intent on imparting static skills upon a generation that should be preparing for an ever-changing world. I'd rather my kids know how to logically dig through a database for answers and connections than engage in pointless rote memorization. I want them to understand how to *use* information, not just how to recite it. I don't want them to just memorize the Gettysburg Address. I want them to really understand the meaning behind the words. My hope for my kids is that their education provides them with a platform of information that comes in handy when they're working to fulfill their God mission, whatever that may be.

In her bestselling and groundbreaking book, *The Smartest Kids in the World*, author Amanda Ripley takes a look at education around the world to discover why some countries that spend less than the US does on public education have seemingly better outcomes. She follows the cultural and classroom experiences of three American high school students—hailing from Oklahoma, Minnesota, and Pennsylvania—who are studying abroad in Finland, Korea, and Poland.

As part of her research for the book, Ripley interviewed the head of a large corporation. She writes, "In Oklahoma, the CEO of the company that makes McDonald's apple pies told me that she had trouble finding enough Americans to handle modern factory jobs during a recession. The days of rolling out dough and packing pies in a box were over. She needed people who could read, solve problems and communicate what had happened on their shift, and there weren't enough of them coming out of Oklahoma's high schools and community colleges."[4]

Good readers.

Problem solvers.

Strong communicators.

Those are the skills that are developed and curated in person-to-person mentoring, not created through more testing.

While education reform or revolution may be what's needed to fix what isn't happening in the classroom, here's the takeaway: We can't depend on schools to be the guiding beacons for our kids. Even if we've found an ideal academy for our individual child, we still shouldn't expect this. As parents, we need to be on guard against a system or ideology or process becoming an ideal. That doesn't work if we want to raise an original.

The truth is, there's no one educational philosophy that has a stronger ability to accomplish God's purpose for our kids. We can dig in on an educational approach, but that approach can miss completely if it doesn't work for our child. I've seen homeschoolers doggedly stay the course, even when it's clearly not working for their family. I've seen public schoolers refuse to entertain other options, even when their kids are withering in the system. I've seen private schoolers valiantly defend their schooling choice, even when the school's learning approach is making mincemeat of their child's self-esteem.

As believing parents, we need to quit "believing" in one type of educational system or another and instead believe in allowing God to direct our steps in figuring out the best approach for our original kid.

While we are the beneficiaries of living in an era in which information and education have expanded, God has long been involved in the learning processes of His people. And He's often used that educational background in a far different way than the professors and teachers of those students might have imagined. God's involvement in the education of His purpose-called people often gets reconfigured in the story of their lives, in the fulfillment of their true selves, and in the carrying out of the assignments He has for them.

FIRST BABY

Once upon a time, a child—who we will call First Baby—was born into an unfortunate time and place. Years before, his ancestors had entered a foreign country, driven there by drought and famine in their homeland. At first, the hungry tribe was welcomed as honored guests. But as the years and then decades and eventually centuries clicked by, their gracious hosts forgot their manners and enslaved the guests, who had long since forgotten their identity as God's chosen people.

By the time First Baby was born, the slave population was booming. But living conditions were terrible, and the slave masters became nervous that the slaves would revolt. So they hatched a plan to kill every baby boy born to the slaves in order to control the population and preserve their own authority.

First Baby's mother could see threads of destiny and purpose woven throughout his fresh existence. And she realized that the execution squad might be on its way at any moment. For a while, she successfully secreted away the baby at home. But as he grew and gurgled and smiled, she knew it was only a matter of time before she heard that knock on the door and he was taken away from her.

In a stroke of desperation—and, as it turned out, genius—
she fashioned him an aquatic car seat and deposited him on the
main thoroughfare of the region—a river. She had his big sister
stand by, watching and waiting for faith, ingenuity, and risk to
intersect.

There's a remarkable collection of wisdom writings called the
Midrash. These texts come alongside the Tanakh—the Hebrew
Bible—and fill in the details of biblical passages, somewhat like
our modern-day commentaries. While I wouldn't say every opinion offered in the Midrash should be regarded as from the mind
of God, it does offer beautiful context and poetic trivia in concert
with biblical texts. It's from the Midrash that a name comes bub-
bling up from the depths of history—a name for the next player
to enter this stage of baby and river and gamble.

Batyah.

Daughter of the king, the pharaoh. The one who would discover this buoyant baby, the one who would claim him and protect
him from murderous protocol. The one who would shape his
childhood. The one who would help weave the fiber of the man.

Batyah. Daughter of God.

Batyah takes in First Baby. She names him Moses, which
means "drawn out" in Hebrew and "son of" in Egyptian. And
she raises Moses as her own son. He's not a sociological experiment or her charitable project. He's her *son*.

She gets Moses into the best private schools. It's in the Bible:
"Pharaoh's daughter took him and brought him up as her own
son. Moses was educated in all the wisdom of the Egyptians and
was powerful in speech and action" (Acts 7:21–22).

I could go on and on about my admiration for Batyah, for her
heart and readiness to raise a baby destined for execution. I love
that she equips him with the best scholastic advantage her position
and culture have to offer.

But it's an education that must have seemed pretty pointless for a number of years. And when its purpose finally is revealed, it takes a hard left.

When Moses is forty years old, he gets into serious legal trouble when he takes out a slave master who is abusing a Hebrew slave. He becomes what modern-day law enforcement calls a "flight risk" and hightails it into the wilderness. For the next forty years, despite that stellar Egyptian education and training, Moses becomes an overqualified assistant manager of his father-in-law's shepherding business.

It's there in the wilderness—four decades in—that Moses's birth mother's discernment and his adoptive mother's investment begin to reveal the pattern of their weaving. God, dabbling in pyrotechnics and botany, reveals Himself to Moses through an ignited shrub. He tells Moses to return to Egypt and free the slave race. And that's where that premier Egyptian education gets dusted off. It becomes background and intel for the culture and government into which Moses will speak. It gives Moses a unique perspective into the upcoming negotiation experience.

But that education is not Moses's purpose. It's not his calling. He never becomes the pharaoh or the pharaoh's governor or prime minister or golf buddy. And it's not the thing that equips him for what God has called him do. God has to do quite a bit of confidence therapy with Moses—getting him to Toastmasters, recruiting big brother Aaron to act as a Cyrano de Bergerac to Moses's nervousness and self-doubt. Even with all that fancy education in his curriculum vitae.

SECOND BABY

Once upon a time, another baby—whom I'll call Second Baby—
was born. His era was one of privilege and power. Technically,
he never should have been the one to take the throne. He had
plenty of older half-brothers with far better claim than he had.
They were the sons birthed from marriages his father had made
for political alliances, for positioning, for networking, for love.

Second Baby's father had spotted his mother when she was still
married to another man. As king, his father exercised his power
to initiate a relationship with the very beautiful and very married
woman. A pregnancy resulted, and a successful murder—as well
as an unsuccessful cover-up—ensued.

A baby was born.

A baby who would not survive.

The next baby born of this couple would survive, a child born
with the residue of scandal and mourning smudging his heritage.
And he would bypass the usual line of succession to the throne.

Second Baby becomes king. Not because he had been groomed
for it. Not because he had a rightful claim. Not because he had
completed his monarchy degree with honors.

That baby—Solomon—became king over Israel because God
chose him to be king. His father, David, explains: "Of all my
sons—and the LORD has given me many—he has chosen my son
Solomon to sit on the throne of the kingdom of the LORD over
Israel" (1 Chronicles 28:5). David goes on to acknowledge that
Solomon hasn't been educated, hasn't been trained for this massive
undertaking, this ruling of Israel and the building of the temple.
David says, "My son Solomon, the one whom God has chosen, is
young and inexperienced" (1 Chronicles 29:1).

Now, David isn't trying to sabotage Solomon here. Not in any
way. He's simply validating that God's calling isn't contingent on

preparation, education, or grooming. God may use those things, but He doesn't have to.

When Solomon takes the throne after his father's death, God then takes up the issue of Solomon's education. And he does it in one of the most efficient ways possible. God appears to Solomon and tells him to ask for whatever he wants. Solomon answers, "You have shown great kindness to David my father and have made me king in his place. Now, LORD God, let your promise to my father David be confirmed, for you have made me king over a people who are as numerous as the dust of the earth. Give me wisdom and knowledge, that I may lead this people, for who is able to govern this great people of yours?" (2 Chronicles 1:8–10).

God grants that request and then some, giving Solomon a full download of all knowledge and wisdom available along with a fully stocked bank account. For a long time, I thought that Solomon was specifically given *spiritual* knowledge and wisdom, and I do think that was part of the package. But God also gave him a law degree so he could have wisdom and discernment in dispensing judgment. And degrees in zoology and botany: "He spoke about plant life, from the cedar of Lebanon to the hyssop that grows out of walls. He also spoke about animals and birds, reptiles and fish" (1 Kings 4:33). Finally, God seems to have granted Solomon degrees in music and literature, as the wise king penned 3,000 proverbs and wrote lyrics for more than 1,000 songs.

The education God provided Solomon became one of the hallmarks of his reign. His education was a beautiful, powerful thing—a tool that helped him to rule and to rule successfully. But it was a tool, not a calling. It was a gear in his purpose, not a guarantee.

THIRD BABY

Once upon a time, another child—Third Baby—was born. He was born into a time in which his country was under foreign rule and religion was floundering and defensive. His educational route was excellent. He was most likely reading by age five or six, memorizing and writing Jewish Scripture by age ten, and was shipped off in his early teens to Jerusalem to study with Gamaliel, the leading Jewish professor of his time.

Paul.

He was educated in every aspect of Jewish theology and hermeneutics. Some who have studied his education speculate he was being trained for a high level of Jewish leadership. Paul says of his training, "I was advancing in Judaism beyond many of my own age among my people and was extremely zealous for the traditions of my fathers" (Galatians 1:14).

So quickly was Paul's star rising that he was present in an official capacity when the Sanhedrin—that exclusive group of Jewish intellects who served as the Hebrew Supreme Court and Legislature—boldly hauled vocal Christian convert Stephen out of court and stoned him. Paul was educationally, politically, and positionally poised to enjoy a successful career in the most prestigious Semitic circles.

Until.

He unexpectedly, dramatically, and blindly was called to a far different path. Jesus reached out to Paul, and Paul responded. Paul became the Lord's chosen instrument.

But catch this.

If I were doing job recruitment—granted, very dramatic job recruitment—for Jesus, I'd be looking at the scholastic records and aligning that schooling with the job I selected for someone. Not Jesus. He says of Paul, "This man is my chosen instrument to proclaim my name to the *Gentiles* and their kings" (Acts 9:15, emphasis added). Not the Jews. Not the group he's been specifically educated to interact with.

True, Paul will occasionally show off that sterling Jewish catechism before his own people, but he'll primarily speak, love, debate, and lead those tolerated enemies of the Jews, the Romans. And he will go on to say of his own calling, "They recognized that I had been entrusted with the task of preaching the gospel to the uncircumcised, just as Peter had been to the circumcised. For God, who was at work in Peter as an apostle to the circumcised, was also at work in me as an apostle to the Gentiles" (Galatians 2:7–8).

The question here is, *why?*

Why would God choose to not leverage that Gamaliel-gilded education of Paul's and put it to work converting the Jews?

Paul himself answers the question when he tells the church at Corinth, "I came to you in weakness with great fear and trembling. My message and my preaching were not with wise and persuasive words, but with a demonstration of the Spirit's power, so that your faith might not rest on human wisdom, but on God's power (1 Corinthians 2:3–4).

THE PURPOSE OF EDUCATION

If you've ever wondered if there's a risk that younger kids in a big family will get lost in the crowd, my sixth child, Journey, will assuage your fears.

Precocious and hilarious, she's been keeping pace with the big kids her whole life. When big sister Madison declared one of her college majors, Journey, five years old at the time, piped up that she too had selected a major of her own.

"I am going to major," she proclaimed, allowing for a dramatic pause to build suspense, "in . . . British Accent. I'm already really good at it! Watch this . . . *Good day, old chap!* See?! And I'm going to minor in Leprechaun!"

I love that Journey already looks at a university experience as something to enhance what she already enjoys, something to develop what she's already good at: performing. And being hilarious. And acting pretty goofy.

Is there a degree for that?

But, really. What about that? Instead of holding up a college degree as keeper of our destiny, what if we simply viewed it as a tool to enhance our purpose?

Back to Mississippi.

Back to my dad's history.

Back to the red dirt, the fickle farm, the young man who gazed at the stars and grabbed hold of a university education. The professional who designed systems that accessed the celestial.

Back to the most important part of the story.

My dad's education helped fuel his dreams because his real learning began with his relatively uneducated but incredibly wise parents. He was nurtured on integrity. He saw modeled and was taught an incredible work ethic. He was encouraged to dream big. His greatest success was not that he trafficked in the galaxy but that he did his work as a man of God—with honesty, excellence, creativity, and heart. Those qualities that had been seeded and cultivated in him ultimately made his education effective. My grandparents saw in my father inventiveness and curiosity. They saw he was a pragmatic dreamer.

I think back on my grandmother's incredible garden, her willingness to honor the unique characteristics of each plant, to intuit the various conditions and soil requirements and nutrients it needed. I see that same garden wisdom played out in the way my grandparents raised my dad. Without the encouragement and adoration of his parents, without their common sense lessons on valuing others, sharing, telling the truth, and working hard, my dad's hard-won degrees would have fallen short of their intended purpose.

To embrace you for the original you are, to impart character and integrity, and then to make sure you know how to spell and where to put your commas? Well, that seems to be the best educational plan of all.

Recalibrate your understanding of education. Recalibrate your expectations about what education can do. Submit any preconceived notions about educational approach and assumption of best practices. Consider first who your child is, how she learns, where she shines. Education is one of several tools to be placed in a box of resources of preparation; it's not the container of all potential, all destiny, all future. Your child is the container. God is the orchestrator of your child's future. Not the admissions counselor. Not an SAT score. Let's always remind our kids—and ourselves—that God is the One in charge of the report card that really matters.

CHAPTER 5

IT'S NOT JUST ABOUT PROTECTING THEM

As parents we have a tendency to overprotect;
it's okay to try and show them all positives but
we cannot forget that the real world has teeth.

Johnnie Dent Jr.

IT WAS WHEN we got into the car to bring her home from the hospital.

That's when it hit.

That's when I felt it.

The fear.

It slammed my heart with a force almost as altering as the love that had just taken up residence there—love for this brand-new baby girl who had been placed in our keeping and care.

It left me equally dizzy and breathless.

The fear.

I hadn't had what I'd call a fearful pregnancy with our oldest child, Madison. Actually, it was quite the opposite. With that first-time experience in the prenatal, I was blissful and clueless, happily round and naive, waddling toward my due date. I strolled into the birth center a few hours after my water broke, figuring we'd be able to check out shortly with an infant in tow.

Which was pretty much how it turned out . . .

. . . after thirty-one hours of labor and some rather unsavory moments.

Which may or may not have involved some highly undignified attempts to speed up labor as well as a fourth-degree episiotomy.

I digress.

When we placed Madison, swathed in blankets and harnessed in her huge car seat, in the back of our little Ford Escort and merged onto the expressway to take her back to our townhouse, it felt like every vehicle on the road was heading in a direct line for us. The sky looked gloomy. The city that had seemed so sparkling the morning we'd driven to the birth center now looked cheerless and menacing.

And the expressway wasn't all I was worried about.

Germs.

And bacteria.

And viruses.

It was as if I could now see those things, as if somehow, through the process of birthing a baby, I'd also been granted some kind of microscopic super vision that could discern ephemeral virulence. I'd never been a germophobe, and yet pathogens were now perceptible.

And they all looked like fear.

We arrived back at our little townhouse, the abode I thought I'd left shining and hygienic. But two feet inside the front door with that fresh, innocent newborn, and I was ready to bleach every possible surface. Also, some of the neighbors now seemed sinister. And the carpet really gross. And the locks on the doors and windows inadequate.

I was afraid.

Very afraid.

My world had shifted as I held this tiny little person who seemed so fragile and vulnerable. I felt like I was the only thing standing between her and the big, bad world.

That responsibility seemed an incredibly tenuous and overwhelming load.

A UNIVERSAL CONDITION

I recently posted a request on Facebook asking for parenting topics that people would like to see covered in a blog I write for a Christian radio station. I purposely left the request open-ended, not suggesting specific categories.

The responses went a little something like this . . .

I'm really afraid that . . .
My concerns for my kids are . . .
In a world that's increasingly dark, my biggest fear for my child is . . .

Regardless of what came after that . . . , fear was always the precursor. Not, *I'd love some suggestions on managing technology.* Or, *How do you handle dating in your family?* Nada from the active voice.

Nope.

Almost every concern started with fear.

Reactive.

Afraid.

Understandably, fear comes home to roost with this parenting thing. Some of us already struggle with an anxious nature long before we become parents. Some discover worry to be our new anti-BFF after the baby comes. But most of us, one way or another, find a cord of disquiet entwined around our hearts, squeezing in spurts and stops, pulsing with flickers of fright and worst-case scenarios.

And our usual technique for attempting to calm our fears is

actually anything but calming—it's controlling. We try to control everything that comes our kid's way. We try to control outcomes. Experiences. Circumstances in all their minutiae.

What we're really trying to control is our fear.

But we're only feeding it.

And fear, once fed, grows.

In our desire to protect, we rapidly veer into extremes. We use antibacterial hand gel as body lotion. We buffer the emotional impact of any tragic story with a line-by-line analysis of how it could have been prevented. We attempt to encase our neighborhood, our church, our community, in a cushion of predictability. We call it preventative. We believe if we power our way ahead of time through any potential unpleasantness, we can plow a path that is painless. Carefree. Innocent. The very theme park of privileged childhood.

Psychologists have labeled this parenting style—and you're probably familiar with the term—*helicopter parenting*. These are the parents who have hovered and hand-wrung and harassed every situation their child has encountered into a pulverized pulp of contrived comfort. These kids arrive at the threshold of adulthood without knowing how to operate a washing machine. They've never darkened the door of a grocery store solo. They have no clue how to keep a checkbook, a calendar, or any accountability. They can't communicate their way through conflict. Their seamless, concierge'd life has prepared them for little apart from wishes granted and everything going perfectly according to plan.

Psychologist Chris Meno of Indiana University warns about the long-term effects of helicopter parenting: "The fruits of parental over-involvement include higher levels of anxiety and depression among adult children. When children aren't given the space to struggle through things on their own, they don't learn to problem-solve very well. They don't learn to be confident in their own abilities, and it can affect their self-esteem. The other problem with never having to struggle is that you never experience failure and can develop an overwhelming fear of failure and of disappointing others. Both the low self-confidence and the fear of failure can lead to depression or anxiety."[5]

Kids seem to have two responses to parents who, operating out of fear, are trying to bubble-wrap their children. Some grow more fretful, more fearful, more sensitive, because that's what Mom and Dad are modeling. Others push back and rebel and engage in crazy risk-taking, attempting to shake off the remnants of a cushioned, overly protected upbringing.

We've created the tangle. We've unwittingly set the trap. Wrapped in the strings of unreality and cushioned by pillows of non-consequence, our kids find themselves entangled in lack of experience. Tangled in naiveté. And, if we've really wound the bubble wrap tightly, they'll find themselves encased in selfishness and self-agenda as well.

Curious threads can't breathe in bubble wrap. It suffocates the spark right out of them.

CONTAGIOUS

I thought that successive pregnancies and babies would inoculate me from the fear monster, but that wasn't the case. While I'm outwardly a very laid-back mom, my inner dialogue can be full of some crazy angst.

Just sixteen months after the birth of our second child, McKenna, we found ourselves surprised to be pregnant yet again. I was currently in the middle of a huge music project and had been working out like a fiend to lose the baby weight I'd gained with McKenna. Michael was up to his eyeballs building a business and the timing of this pregnancy—in our eyes—couldn't have been worse. Being a busy mom, I'd lost track of where I was in my cycle and realized one day, while waiting for my daughter's dance class to finish, that I was late by a couple of weeks. I hightailed it to the drugstore across the street from the dance studio and grabbed a cellophane-wrapped pregnancy test, tossing the money at the clerk. Then I sprinted back to the studio, made a beeline for the restroom, went through the test steps, and analyzed the evidence.

Positive.

Glaringly positive.

God forgive me, I cried and cried, frustrated and worried about the impact this pregnancy would have on my music project and on our finances.

It took me a couple of weeks, but I finally accepted this change of plans, and by the time we went in for our first ultrasound, I was happy and excited to see baby number three, heart thrumming, limbs waving. I'd already moved up to the next size in clothes, and my energy level was returning.

One afternoon while I was working in the recording studio, I took a quick decaf coffee and restroom break. I was surprised to note that I was spotting a bit, but the amount was quite negligible. Making a mental note to mention it to the doctor at my next appointment, I went back into the studio to finish up the session.

Another week or so clicked by and before I knew it, I was entering my second trimester. I got out of bed one night and was stunned to discover I was spotting again, much heavier this time. The next morning I hurried into the doctor's office, baby McKenna on my hip, a little worried but trying to reassure myself that lots of women I knew had spotted during their pregnancies and everything had turned out just fine. At the doctor's office, everything was still measuring normally, so we went in to the ultrasound room to get a quick look.

Where it was revealed that my womb had gone silent.

The baby's heart had stopped beating.

I drove home in a blur of tears . . . and guilt . . . and anger . . . and sadness.

The baby I had been annoyed was on the way was now the baby I couldn't bear to lose.

And yet I would.

The following days were a bewildering mix of waiting and flurry, not knowing at what point my body would fully begin the miscarriage process. Ultimately, my body didn't want to give the baby up, so I ended up going in for surgery. Throat aching from the embedded knot of grief, I signed the necessary paperwork, including signing away the baby's body since we were early in the second trimester.

Michael and I wrestled with our hearts in the following weeks, sorting through our emotions, looking for the lessons to be learned. We repented. We cried. We were keenly aware of the sweetness and life of our two little girls and sadly aware of the emptiness of my womb. We were tempted to take permanent measures to avoid going through this again, to prevent any possibility of future pregnancies. But something within each of us felt a push, a longing to give it one more go. The excitement that had ultimately developed in that unexpected third pregnancy had left us realizing we could indeed welcome another child into our little family of four.

We explored the idea of adopting. Requesting information from adoption agencies, we began that conversation. And, though we were still uncertain, we prayed about another pregnancy.

Six months after the miscarriage, we were pregnant again.

And this time, my response was not joy or frustration.

It was fear.

A fear that would occupy the many days that made up my pregnancy.

Fear sat mockingly on my shoulder, a black raven of a thing, feathers glistening, sharp beak ready to poke my bruised heart, claws ready to clutch my mind and dig in their barbs of alarm.

When I found out we were having a boy, fear mocked me as I began what should have been the joyful experience of planning his nursery.

Fear giggled malevolently when I bought little boy outfits.

Fear had a field day when I started spotting.

Fear smirked when the spotting stopped, turning temporary relief into a sense of foreboding.

Fear trounced me thoroughly.

I worried over Justus. I fretted. I was thrilled when he was born, and I was terrified. I worried that if I didn't worry, it would usher in something real to be worried about.

Justus was the fussiest of my babies. He startled easily. He cried often. And he was attached solely to me. With huge blue eyes and the craziest triple cowlick you've ever seen right at the center of his forehead, he was my biggest fan and my most devoted barnacle. He clung to me, tagged after me, stalked me.

He flunked out of preschool at the age of three.

True story.

For sixth months, he cried every time I dropped him off at preschool. He even tried to leave the building and come find me during naptime. He kept crying. He wouldn't eat his lunch. After half a year of agony, the course was clear.

Justus was a Rainbow School dropout.

The autumn he was seven, we spent the day after Thanksgiving at Silver Dollar City outside of Branson, Missouri. Silver Dollar City is a beautiful amusement park located in the Ozark Mountains. With live music shows and just enough roller coasters to keep things interesting, the park's hilly, tree-lined paths were decked out in full fall glory with a leaf carpeting of gold, crimson, and copper. The scent of hot chocolate and funnel cakes perfumed the air with the very incense of heaven. By this point, we had six children, the youngest being Journey, a four-month-old baby.

The park was fully decked out to welcome the Christmas season. Carolers strolled the paths, harmonic blends of Yuletide favorites the soundtrack for the day. As if on cue, a light snow began to fall, turning the entire vista magical. The day was crisp, not cold enough to be miserable but chilly enough to justify swilling hot chocolate at every beverage station. Michael and most of the bigger kids raced from ride to ride, joy and glee oozing from every pore. I followed behind with the double stroller, pushing two-year-old Jairus and baby sister Journey, delighting in the excitement of the day. At dusk, Christmas lights illuminated every tree, every ride, every shop, and the enormous tree at the center of the park was scheduled to be lit with tremendous fanfare.

For most of my family, the day was utterly perfect.

Except.

For Justus, Silver Dollar City might have well been Sinister Darkness City.

From the moment we walked through the gates, Justus was glued to me. He was terrified someone would try to steal the stroller with the babies in it. He freaked out when Michael ran ahead with the other kids to get in line for a ride. He sprinted ahead, trying to coerce them to come back, as he anxiously looked over his shoulder to make sure I was still in sight. He worried over the mechanical conditions of the various rides. He constantly checked to make certain I hadn't left the diaper bag behind. He worried that the new baby might be too cold, even though Journey was snuggled warmly against me in a cozy baby carrier. He refused to try any of the rides. He panicked about sister Maesyn's hearing aids getting wet when it began to snow.

In his fear, he was exhausting.

And exhausted.

Toward the end of the day, Michael asked if I wanted to go on one of the rides. I've always loved roller coasters, but so far I'd been too busy nursing Journey and getting everyone fed and be-mittened. I jumped at the chance and headed for one of the coasters just a few minutes before the park was scheduled to close. Justus quickly announced that he would ride with me, which surprised us as he'd steadfastly refused to ride anything fast the whole day. The closer we got to the front of the line, the more anxious and upset Justus became. Tears filled his eyes, and he was breathing fast. I kept telling him he didn't have to ride, but he was resolute.

Justus and I climbed into the roller coaster and strapped on our safety belts. He frantically checked every buckle, telling me over and over that he loved me. The ride began and Justus's face was a frozen mask of fear, lips peeled back from his teeth, eyes wide and terrified. As roller coasters go, this one was pretty mild, but you'd never have known it from Justus's countenance. His was a portrait of sheer panic.

After some swirls and loops and drops, the roller coaster came skidding back into the entry shed. We disembarked and walked toward the rest of the family, the other kids laughing and clapping. Justus, hand tucked firmly in mine, turned to me and said, "Well, that went better than I thought. I really thought we were going to die."

He wasn't trying to be funny.

That sweet boy, that little worrywart of a guy, was willing to go with me into what he thought was assured mutual destruction because his fear of being without me was greater than his fear of that terrifying roller coaster.

It was then that I knew.

Fear is contagious.

My anxiousness and worry throughout my pregnancy and his

babyhood, along with his more sensitive bent, had tangled into a panicked perspective. Even though I thought I hadn't allowed my jitters to creep over into his psyche, I had.

I discovered something about myself as well. Because fear can be contagious, I too had caught it. I come from a family line that's made worry, fear, and anxiety an art form. It all came from a place of love. From a place of responsibility and caring and heart. But it was fear, all the same.

Nothing makes you realize the need for a fear-ectomy like watching a seven-year-old kid whose fear prevents him from enjoying a glorious day at the amusement park. After watching him struggle so mightily that day, I realized that Michael and I would need to help Justus push past fear, that we'd need to stop editing every experience in a misplaced effort to keep him from anxiety. And that meant I would need to model a life not limited by fear and avoidance. I would need to show my son how to navigate worry and stress.

The poet king, David, knew what it was like to have the raven of fear clamped upon his shoulder. He knew what it was like to cringe at its malevolent babbling and its hissing whispers. He knew what it was like to feel the dread snake twist around his heart. So he wrote. He sang. He penned his process of starving fear, of moving from paralyzed panic to unfettered faith. It's a template that still holds true today, a model that would help Justus and me run our fingertips across the features of faith.

> When hard pressed, I cried to the LORD;
>   he brought me into a spacious place.
> The LORD is with me; I will not be afraid.
>   What can mere mortals do to me?
> The LORD is with me; he is my helper.
>   I look in triumph on my enemies.

It is better to take refuge in the LORD
  than to trust in humans.
It is better to take refuge in the LORD
  than to trust in princes . . .

I was pushed back and about to fall,
  but the LORD helped me.
The LORD is my strength and my defense;
  he has become my salvation.
                    Psalm 118: 5–9, 13–14

Fast-forward eleven years. The Rainbow School dropout, the
kid who was terrified at the amusement park—that guy answered
a call to go to Africa. To Uganda. And he was scared. He was
anxious that he wouldn't get the money raised. He was worried
about traveling internationally. Although his team was going to
the eastern region of Africa, the Ebola virus was raging in western
parts of the continent. He was concerned about the safety of his
sister and his friends, who were also going on the trip.

And he went anyway.

He owned up to the emotion of fear. He talked about it with
the lead pastor on the trip. And he started starving the fear, not
allowing it to spread to his mission partners.

He didn't allow fear to limit his life.

And his mama? This gal?

A few days before the team left, my pastor asked me if I was
nervous. If I was concerned. If I was a little bit freaked out. I
told him that I was refusing to allow myself to ask any of those
questions.

My son needed me to be brave. He needed me to not pull out
the bubble wrap. So, by God's grace and King David's template,
that's what I did.

I did it so Justus could fly. So he could live a bigger life. So he could have his heart a little bit broken by the orphans he was serving. So that in the breaking, his heart could become even bigger, its borders stretched to include those precious African children living in the streets of Kampala.

We're making progress, he and I.

Progress toward starving fear.

Progress toward trusting God.

THE FEAR FABLE

Part of our problem with bubble wrap and helicoptering comes from the fantasy we Western parents have created about childhood. We shield our kids from talk of disease and war and mortality and sexual misconduct and general unpleasantness. We verbalize how we wish the world were more innocent like it was for past generations, essentially ignoring the truths history had recorded about those generations.

I adored—still adore, actually—Laura Ingalls Wilder's books based on her childhood growing up in a homesteading pioneer family in the American Midwest. I read all of them, cover to cover, over and over throughout my own childhood. Laura's delightful accounts of baking with Ma and listening to Pa play the fiddle seem to be the stuff of simpler, gentler times. Her stories paint a portrait of sweet youth, anchored in home and family, one-room schoolhouse and church. But when I began rereading the books to my own children, I had a startling revelation. Laura Ingalls Wilder's childhood was hard. Really hard. There between the stories of patchwork quilt sewing and butter churning are the details of a family stripped of their homestead claim, of devastating illness that cost sister Mary her eyesight, of blizzards and robbery. Many times the cupboard was bare, the crops failed, and debt soared. I had gotten so caught up in the romance of the plains, petticoats, and ponies of the West that I hadn't realized just how desperate Laura's childhood had been at times.

To say that the remarkable Laura Ingalls Wilder was the product of a protected, innocent, romanticized childhood would be to dishonor the strength, courage, and faith that carried her through hard times. For most of the world's children throughout time, carefree childhood was a myth. And while I certainly want my kids to look back on their younger years with joy and happiness and celebration, I also know the value of difficult experiences, frustrating challenges, and overwhelming pressure.

It's important to realize when we're veering into helicopter hovering and mom-driven or dad-driven micromanaging. We need to be wary of laying a cushioned and silk-tangled trap of ease and entitlement for our kids. And we need to be honest.

So check in with a trusted friend or your parenting partner when you're feeling unsure. And watch for some things yourself. Take note if you're already somewhat anxious. If you struggle with allowing your kids to fail. If you see your kids as younger than they actually are. If you consistently intervene on their behalf with teachers and coaches and playmates. Those cautionary flashes remind us to ease up and back off.

THE STRENGTH IS IN THE STRUGGLE

Michael and I celebrated our 25th wedding anniversary in 2014 and went on what we called our Silver Honeymoon. We headed to a beautiful beach resort close to where we went on our original honeymoon and enjoyed several gorgeous days of rest and sunshine.

On one of our final evenings at the resort, we were sprawled on beach chairs, watching the sky move from shades of blue to a kaleidoscope of orange and pink and gold as the sun began to slide down the horizon. From the corner of my eye, I saw several resort employees making their way down toward the surf, carrying a large plastic tub. Curious, I sat up in my chair. Michael, also curious, got up and walked down to where they were, then motioned for me to join him.

Nestled in the plastic tub were about 150 baby sea turtles, newly hatched that afternoon.

The area of the Caribbean where we were staying is a natural sea turtle nesting area. Our resort, in cooperation with a natural preservation program, monitors the beach for sea turtle nests, protects those nests, and—once the baby sea turtles hatch—helps the babies get off to a strong start by releasing them into the ocean.

It was a powerful example of how humans can protect and participate in the processes of nature.

Plus, baby sea turtles are ridiculously cute.

Ridiculously.

Like, really.

My maternal heart gave a flip as I watched them move their little flippers and clamber over their fellow turtle siblings still snuggled in the towel-lined plastic crate. Miniature and geometric, their small shells were a gorgeous pattern of deep tannish greens, tiny tiles set in ornate, exact patterns. The resort employees had set the crate about twenty feet up the beach from the surf, and the baby turtles were already pushing toward the side of the crate that faced the seawater, their sense of the ocean as home already in full operation.

And then, as the sun dropped lower in the sky, one of the resort workers called to me. As I walked toward him, he gestured to the crate and motioned for me to pick up one of those amazingly teensy turtles.

Me?

Really?

Vacation trip made. Right there.

I cautiously picked up one ambitious guy who was trying to scale the side of the crate. Flippers waving, small head craning toward the sea, he felt cool and smooth, the soft leather of his belly and shell a delightful new texture in my hands. I couldn't believe how strong he was for such a tiny creature. His flippers rasped against my palms, the drive for motion and waves creating his choreography.

I named him Abraham.

He looked like an Abraham. In a turtle kind of way.

The director of the release program drew a long line in the sand, marking the starting point for the upcoming journey. He explained that the turtles needed to make their own way down to the water, that we were not to carry them to the surf. We then began to pick up Abraham's siblings from the crate and set them on the sand at that line, heads facing the sea. By then, a few other resort guests had made their way over to our impromptu zoological lesson and joined us in placing babies on the sand. As if a horn had sounded to start the race, little turtles began scrambling toward the waves, scaling big clumps of seaweed and pushing their way through uneven sand. Some reached the water quickly; others moved at a more leisurely pace.

A few got a little confused.

A few stopped.

I set Abraham down at the line and his odyssey to the ocean began. His nose sniffing the salty air, he made a beeline for the surf, tiny flippers churning up grains of sand, a distinctive trail in his wake. I walked to the water alongside him, mindful to honor the boundaries. I clapped, I cheered, and yes, I'm not ashamed to admit that I got a little teary as I saw that tiny turtle scoot into the water and tumble into the tide.

In the rush of my sudden turtle love, I uttered a little prayer that God would protect Abraham throughout his life and carry him into full adulthood. Yes, I cried over a baby turtle and became a turtle prayer warrior, all in one fell swoop.

It was just profound to see this intricate and pocket-sized being launch himself into the vastness of a turbulent ocean.

I turned from seeing Abraham successfully dispatched into the surf to find more baby turtles making their way through the sand. Most of us onlookers were standing back, watching the varying levels of success and struggle. A few of the turtles seemed exhausted, overwhelmed by the challenges of the terrain. Others got turned around, heading away from the sea or scrambling in a parallel line to the water. We watched, a little worried, until dusk began to settle. Finally, one of the resort guests couldn't take it anymore. She scooped up one of the stragglers and began to carry him down to the water, unable to bear the uncertainty. One of the employees in charge of the release called after her, motioning for her to put the turtle down, but her overwhelming concern overshadowed his instructions. As she gently placed the turtle in the shallows, her husband caught up with her and reminded her that she wasn't supposed to help the turtles. She, on the other hand, was incredulous that we were allowing these turtles to struggle so mightily. She saw her actions as a kindness.

Unwittingly, though, she was participating in potentially tangling the turtle population in protective bubble wrap.

That trip from the sand to the water? That's critical turtle training ground. It's what gives baby turtles a better chance of survival. The best conditions possible had been created by monitoring the nest and timing the release at sunset when predatory birds and scavengers are not as active. But once those conditions had been achieved, newly hatched turtles need the trek to the water to strengthen their flippers, to practice the motion that will be required once they hit the water. They need the experience of heading accurately toward the shore, even if it takes them a bit to figure it out. These moments of struggle in the sands of their childhood would serve them well during their next hundred years of survival. What an overprotective heart saw as too hard or too cruel or too tough is actually exactly what a baby turtle needed to up his chances of survival. To cut the journey short, to abbreviate the endeavor, would make the turtles more vulnerable and compromise their skills for endurance.

> **THE STRENGTH IS IN THE STRUGGLE.**

The strength is in the struggle.

Hard as it can be to watch. Fearful as it can make us.

Fear, when fed, grows.

Once fear grows, it becomes contagious.

And once it becomes contagious, it can limit the scope of a life.

But we can't let that happen.

Even when it seems easier to scoop up a struggling sea turtle and carry it down to the shore.

Even when it seems easier to intervene in every schoolyard conflict.

Even when it seems easier to protect and buffer and bubble wrap and round off all the sharp edges of life.

Even then.

When I was recently interviewed by the national radio program *Keep the Faith*, I was asked what my biggest fear was when it came to my kids. I hadn't had access to the interview questions ahead of time and therefore hadn't really considered what I would say. I fumbled a bit, saying I thought most parents worried about their children's safety and their futures. As my mind raced for a cogent answer, all of a sudden it was there.

"I think my greatest fear is that I would allow my fear to somehow limit my kids, that my fear would hold them back from their purpose and destiny," I told the interviewer. I was confessing and teaching and reminding myself all at the same time. It was one of those moments in which you know the Holy Spirit is telling you something. It's the one thing we should appropriately fear as parents, that we would limit our kids' destinies because of our own fears.

> FEAR, WHEN FED, GROWS. ONCE FEAR GROWS, IT BECOMES CONTAGIOUS. AND ONCE IT BECOMES CONTAGIOUS, IT CAN LIMIT THE SCOPE OF A LIFE.

It's time to land the helicopter. It's time to untangle the snares of fear. It's time to tell the raven to get off our shoulder. It's time to starve the fear monster. It's time to trust.

We can never clearly see the threads of purpose in our kids if all we can see is the risk, the scary, the unknown. We can't raise an original if we raise them on a steady diet of worry. For our original kids to reach their full potential, we need to model vision, courage, and daring. We need to show the way. Ask yourself, *Am I parenting in this situation, this challenge, this circumstance, from a place of raising my child's strength and capacity, or am I wrapping him up to defensively buffer my own anxious heart? Am I enabling or empowering?*

Let's end a contagion of fear that spreads its tentacles from one generation to the next. Let's pioneer a new day. Be strong and courageous. Fear not. God commands us to do so (Deuteronomy 31:23). Originality is not the provenance of copy cats and scaredy cats. It's the territory of the brave, the visionary, the bold. Let's let them boldly go.

CHAPTER 6

AND IT'S NOT ABOUT YOU

*You can get tangled up in your own ego of how
you're perceived. You can lose your way.*

Pierce Brosnan

TWENTY-FIVE YEARS AGO, there lived a mom. Deep in the heart of
Texas.

Back in her high school days, she had longed to be a cheerleader.

Now those days were long gone. And she'd never gotten to
don the cute pleated skirt and wave the crackling pompoms. She'd
never gotten to paint her name on the side of a megaphone. She'd
never stood field side with the cute football players.

What could have been her time had come and gone. And the
yearbook pictures and memory box and heirlooms from her teen
years would never boast of her having been a cheerleader.

But now she had a second chance.

She now had a daughter, who was of age to begin her own
cheerleading career.

The mom had been preparing her daughter for this time. The
girl had been enrolled in gymnastics classes and cheer training at
an early age. From the time she'd been in preschool, her mom had

dressed her in pint-sized cheer outfits. Surely this next generation of cheerleading aspiration would succeed.

Cheerleader tryouts approached for the junior high squad. Practice upon practice was held. The day finally arrived.

And the daughter didn't make the squad.

This was not acceptable.

This could not be allowed.

When tryouts rolled around the next year, the mom had a plan. A plan she thought would ensure her daughter a place on the squad. A plan that should make her long-held dreams of prestige and popularity come to fruition—through her daughter.

The mom sought the help of an ex-brother-in-law in her insidious scheme. She believed that if the mom of one of her daughter's competitors for a spot on the squad were to die, the trauma would keep the daughter of the victim from trying out.

And then her daughter would take that spot. Her daughter would be a cheerleader.

The ex-brother-in-law recorded his conversations with the desperate mom. Thankfully, he turned those tapes over to the police. The plot was squashed before it could be realized.

The mom went to jail.

And the daughter? In an interview twenty years later, she said that she'd never wanted to be a cheerleader. She'd only trained and tried out to please her mom.[6]

All she'd wanted was to make her mom happy—a happiness that was tethered to an unmet fantasy.

The case of Wanda Holloway rocketed to national headlines in the early 1990s. People were stunned by the level to which someone would go about something as ultimately inconsequential as a junior high cheerleading tryout. And yes, the Holloway case is extreme.

And yet . . .

A 2012 report entitled "Violence in youth sport: Potential preventative measures and solutions"[7] by Cheryl Danilewicz showed
a 10-percent jump in parent violence at youth sporting events in a
five-year span from 1995–2000. Parent violence was defined as parents pushing, shoving, screaming, and fighting with other parents,
coaches, and game officials. By 2008, that number had jumped an
additional 14 percent, bringing witnessed parental physical con-
frontations to a whopping 29 percent at youth sporting events.

I continued to research this issue and was stunned to see the
number of headlines, stories, accounts, and psychological studies
and articles dealing with the subject. As "out there" as Wanda
Holloway's case may seem, unfortunately the core of her story—a
parent overly attached and wrapped up in the identity of her
child—is actually pretty common.

How does this happen? Shouldn't good parents want the very
best for their kids? Don't they want their children to find happiness and have access to more resources than they did? Don't good
parents want their kids to achieve more, go faster, fly higher?

Lisa Firestone, PhD, says in a *Psychology Today* article, "Too
often, we use our children to compensate for our own unmet
goals or limitations. When we don't feel fulfilled in our own
lives, we can over-identify with our kids. In the name of being
'selfless,' we can selfishly lose perspective and focus all our dreams
and desires on them."[8] As Mason Cooley writes, "Self-hatred and
self-love are equally self-centered."

Maybe you've never screamed at a ref or caused a rumble at the
T-ball game, but let's be willing to do an honest self-examination
here. The tangle of self can be insidious and subtle. It can disguise
itself as enthusiasm, pushing for the best, being your kid's advocate. And yet, unchecked and unaware, it can tangle the threads
of a child's temperament to where the identity of the parent and
the destiny of the child become a debilitating snarl.

So what do we need to look for to make sure our own agendas don't get disguised as best intentions? Let's give ourselves some markers to look for, some red flags to place on the field of our parenting to help keep the lines of our lives and the curious threads of our children from being tangled up into a toxic snare.

A TOUGH CHILDHOOD

If you experienced a tough childhood, that's a red flag.

From my work toward my college degree in psychology to my time spent in ministry to everything I've learned about Jesus and His grace, I know that our pasts do not have to define us. They are part of our stories and our testimonies, but they don't have to be the template for our futures.

This is something we need to be very deliberate about. That's because a tough childhood can heavily influence our parenting.

Our lacemaker from the beginning of this book, Zélie, was raised in a restrictive and stern home devoid of affection and laughter. She used the lessons of her past to weave a beautiful future, building a home for her own children that rang with joy and celebration. She lovingly cultivated the individual threads and temperaments of her daughters. But she could have allowed her cold childhood to drive her to a parenting style that was far too permissive as she attempted to soothe her own childhood memories. Or she could have simply fallen back on parenting her daughters the way she'd been raised.

None of us comes through childhood without some bumps and bruises. From playground rejections to sibling conflicts to parental anger to traumatic events—from minor insults to major injuries—everything leaves its mark. Some people have a childhood that was more difficult, more challenging, than most. If that's your story, you may still be working through the rejection, the lack of resources, the fear, the abuse. It's okay to still be finding resolution for those things. But you also need to be aware of how this can affect raising your own children.

We only need to look to the Bible to find someone who had a rough start. Jephthah early on experienced ridicule and rejection, as is recorded in the eleventh chapter of Judges. As his bio goes, Jephthah's dad has a fling with a local prostitute, who becomes pregnant with Jephthah. Dear old dad Gilead is already married to another woman with whom he has several sons. For whatever reason, Jephthah is raised along with his half-brothers, who are quite aware of his splotched pedigree. I imagine Jephthah's childhood is a cruel blend of standing at the edge of family life, never truly fitting in and yet also being known as Gilead's son. After growing up with a passel of half-brothers, Jephthah is driven away from the family lands. His half-brothers want to make sure he isn't going to get a cut of the family wealth when their father dies. They say, "You are not going to get any inheritance in *our* family . . . because you are the son of another woman" (Judges 11:2, emphasis added).

Jephthah takes off, the stinging wind of rejection at his back. He goes to the region of Tob and creates for himself a community of questionable players. This disreputable gang becomes Jephthah's newest band of brothers.

Jephthah's tough childhood does have a side benefit. I imagine him in a testosterone-soaked childhood of half-brothers, usually at the bottom of the dog pile, learning how to fight ferociously. Now, as an uprooted man, his reputation as a scrapper comes back into play. Although his family has kicked him to the curb, they scramble to seek him out when they go up against their nasty neighbors, the Ammonites. The Ammonites have been rattling their sabers, and Gilead's family needs a fighter. So they track down Jephthah and ask him to head up an armed force.

Jephthah has a few questions for them: "Didn't you hate me and drive me from my father's house? Why do you come to me now, when you're in trouble?" (Judges 11:7). His siblings don't bother to apologize, but they do dangle those words that Jephthah longed for throughout his childhood. They tell him if he'll come fight the Ammonites with them, they'll make him head of the family.

Well, now.

That's a turn.

But Jephthah's still feeling like he needs to earn his place, like he must somehow make up for the sin of his father and the profession of his mother. And so he adds a caveat to their offer. If he *defeats* the Ammonites, they can really and truly and for sure make him head of the clan. It's like offering to double the price you're willing to pay for a car after the salesman has already offered you a lower price. His brothers hadn't made a victorious outcome part of the requirement, but Jephthah is trying to prove himself.

Jephthah rounds up his posse and heads out to war. The Bible records that the Spirit of God comes upon him as he makes his journey. He's heading into battle as a strong fighter, with the unexpected confidence of his half-brothers and the promise of becoming head of his family at the conclusion of the conflict.

But Jephthah's childhood of rejection and desperation rears its ugly head again.

As he charges to the front to take on the Ammonites, Jephthah makes a vow to God that he will sacrifice the first thing that walks out his door if he can just have victory over the enemy. It's like he's wanting to pinky promise with God so he can really and truly conquer the Ammonites and be accepted into the family fold. He's trying to bargain with God—and once again upping the price tag when he doesn't have to.

Jephthah soundly defeats the enemy, sacking twenty different towns. Victory complete, he heads home.

Where his vow comes back to haunt him.

The first thing that comes out to greet him is not the family dog. It's not a servant. It's his teenage daughter.

His only child.

She pays the heavy price for her father's unfortunate childhood, his need to overcompensate, his rash vow to God.

Shattered, Jephthah sacrifices his daughter to a God who never asked for such a gesture in exchange for a battle victory.

Whatever unrealized dream, whatever unfairness, whatever trauma you may have experienced in childhood, if the sting of it still hurts, if healing hasn't come, mark that spot clearly. Put light on it. Get some dedicated, qualified help with it, sorting through it with a counselor. And then, with God's help, take out the spiritual tweezers and carefully and cleanly remove the stitches of your wounded past from the open canvas of your child's heart. Don't make your child the sacrifice you're placing on the altar of an unrealized outcome.

A CHARMED CHILDHOOD

If you experienced a charmed childhood, that's a red flag too.

Let me explain.

Every year, I tell myself I won't try to accomplish it again.

And every year I make another attempt at it.

Christmas.

Not just any Christmas, mind you.

The Best Christmas Ever.

My own childhood had its share of difficulties and joys, but one shining star in the middle of it all was Christmas.

My mom and dad knew how to create a charmed Christmas, and there was no experience that compared with Christmas morning.

Huddled secretly in the hallway of our Southern California home on Christmas Eve—when we were supposed to be sound asleep in bed—my brothers Rob and Dave and I would speculate, dream, and hypothesize about what the coming morning would bring. At the slight screech of the hallway pocket door opening, we would scatter like mice, furtively scrambling for our beds, hearts pounding, faking slumber for whichever parent had entered the room to check on us.

We had every reason not to be able to sleep on Christmas Eve, for Christmas morning never disappointed.

As dawn broke, the scent of coffee would perfume the air and it would be time—time to see what awaited us under the tree. We would wait deliriously on the other side of the closed hallway pocket door, ears on high alert, listening for the "okay" signal from my mom.

Skirting the ever-so-hip iron railing that bordered our ever-so-hip sunken living room, we'd clear the step and skid into a euphoria of Noel treasure.

Nothing seemed more amazing. Nothing seemed more satisfying. Presents and candy, music and laughter. Wishes granted and surprises delighted. Magic everywhere. The Christmas tree seemed to stretch higher, the seasonal music on the turntable would soar, and the day would make its watermark once again on my heart.

As we got older—and a little wiser to the ways of Santa Claus—my parents still managed to make the magic. Even when I was in high school and college, my youngest brother, David, remained willing to play the role of reindeer-believing baby of the family, and his enthusiasm was contagious. And right when it would have gotten truly and deeply weird for David to play the role of the excited kid at Christmas, Michael and I had Madison.

A new generation!

Now I would be taking over the office of Chief Christmas Magic Maker!

Net result? I stirred myself into a lumpy crazy sauce trying to recreate the Christmas memories of my youth. I'd bludgeon our tiny budget and ultimately break out the credit cards. I'd bake and scrub and fret and anguish and always feel like I was coming up short and not providing my kids with the same experience I'd had. Of course, I failed to take into consideration the fact that my childhood Christmas memories were experienced *as a child*. My folks did work to make the season special, but I have to laugh at myself when I look back at the home movies and pictures. Through my childhood eyes, it all looked so much bigger and brighter. Processing the anticipation and the surprise and the satisfaction through the eyes of a child made the entire experience take on a high-definition aspect. To try to replicate that feeling as an adult orchestrating the whole thing . . . well, it's the difference between visiting Disney World as a guest and working there behind the scenes. Both great experiences . . . but very different.

For the parent who had the stellar career on the athletic field or in the orchestra, for the mom who found childhood joy in a massive collection of dolls and doll clothes, for the dad who found his groove in debate club and competitions, our tendency can be to try to use the same recipe for success on our kids, to have them do the same things that gild our best memories.

But that may have nothing to do with what's important to our child and what honors the curious threads within them.

Michael and I have friends who have experienced a great deal of financial success. They came from humble beginnings and married young. And they both have remarkable business acumen which, over their course of their three-decade marriage, has resulted in shining careers and fiscal security. They've been able to travel around the world with their kids and educate them in top private schools. They own a variety of gorgeous homes and love Jesus and are very generous.

And smart.

In this way.

They've told their kids to fully enjoy the blessings God has provided for their family, but to also be aware that, as adults, they might not live in the same kind of homes. They might not take the same kind of vacations. They might live simpler lives. And they've told them that it's all good. Their kids need not have an expectation that they'll provide the same luxuries and advantages for their future families. They've made sure their kids know there won't be fat trust funds awaiting them; they want their kids to build their own definition of happiness and success. Which may or may not include the kind of monetary revenue of their childhood. It's not a flippant "money isn't everything" attitude. It's a deliberate detangling of an expectation our society tends to have—that our adulthood will be more prosperous than our childhood.

I love that.

And I'm watching their kids soar. One finding threads that pull him toward a career in business, one serving in the Air Force, one discovering her expression in the arts. They are not encumbered, not feeling pressure to replicate the privileged experiences of their childhoods. They're trusting God to do new things. We don't have to replicate the old, no matter how sweet and fulfilling the memories. And that's the way it should be. We serve a God who is always creating, imagining, crafting. He says, "See, I am doing a new thing! Now it springs up, do you not perceive it?" (Isaiah 43:19).

LOSING TRACK OF YOURSELF

Another red flag to be aware of is losing track of yourself.

In a chapter that so far has dealt with overlaying too much of yourself into your child's life, it may seem a bit surprising to post a red flag on losing track of yourself.

But have you ever tried to untangle a bunch of necklaces? You know how it goes. If you could just find the end of one of the necklaces, you might be able to sort out the whole assortment. But you keep losing track of that one little chain. It keeps getting jumbled back in the bunch, and the tangle remains.

Being crazy about our kids and loving them deeply and investing time and energy and heart in their lives is a great and mighty thing. But some of us become so deeply mired in the lives of our children that we lose our own sense of self. Our personal identity is so wrapped up in our identity as our kids' parent that we lose the thread of us in the weaving. Our perception of ourselves can become one-dimensional. We are the entity known as so-and-so's mom. And that's it.

Congratulations! You've just put the weight of the world on your child's shoulders. You didn't mean to, but by becoming so entangled in your child's life, you've now made their happiness and their hurts your own, and your child has become responsible for your emotions.

Our kids are perceptive. They know when we have no outside interests, no friends, no world that exists outside of them, their activities, and their schedules. They know when we've slipped the backpack of our own selfhood over their shoulders. It pulls at the posture of their own original purpose and adds a dragging weight to their own perception of self. Not only are they now trying to scale the peak of their own future, but they're also carrying us up the mountain as well.

We were not meant to exist attached to the same umbilicus. That curious thread on which we began life was designed to be cut. For some of us, it will take uncommon courage to love our kids more than our own struggle with identity. It will take uncommon courage to slice a clean line.

When I learned I was pregnant with twins—babies number seven and eight for us—I also learned a new word.

Septation.

It's a word used to describe the division of cells and, in a twin pregnancy, it's a word that speaks to each twin being within their own amniotic sac. When you hear the phrase "a strong line of septation," that's a good thing.

> FOR SOME OF US, IT WILL TAKE UNCOMMON COURAGE TO LOVE OUR KIDS MORE THAN OUR OWN STRUGGLE WITH IDENTITY.

Occasionally, twins will develop in the same amniotic sac. They are known as monoamniotic twins, and there are significant risks to the babies in this type of pregnancy. Umbilical cord entanglement or damage can occur, or one twin may become malnourished. Doctors must monitor a multiple pregnancy very carefully when no line of septation is evident.

Whether it's cells, twins, or parents and their kids, a strong line of septation is a healthy thing. Parents so often see their children as a reflection of themselves and so strive to control what that image looks like to the world. They want their communities and peer groups to see them as "normal," so they seek for their children to be seen as "normal" also. While our children are indeed part of us and can resemble us—in appearance or in character—they do need to be "septated" from us. While I was pregnant with my twins, I thought of myself as a Triple Human, an organism supporting three lives. We were a package deal, and yet each of us was a distinct individual.

Families are a package deal, made up of the individual cells of parents and children. As parents, we are painted into the canvas of our children's lives, just as they are painted into ours. But for the health of the family, clearly recognizing the cellular walls of each individual provides the best environment for emotional growth and nourishment.

As Doris Lessing writes in *A Man and Two Women*, "Children can't be a center of life and a reason for being. They can be a thousand satisfying things that are delightful, interesting, satisfying, but they can't be a wellspring to live from. Or they shouldn't be." I sometimes hear a mom say, "I live for my kids." I've probably said it myself. But I belong to Jesus first. I must first live for God and, in the living, raise the kids He's entrusted me with.

A REACTIVE REFLECTION

Our fourth and final red flag is all about a reactive reflection.

Let's go back in the day, as they say.

My mom and I had a longstanding challenge in our mother/daughter relationship.

It had to do with wardrobe. Both color and cut.

Although I have deep Southern roots, there's another kind of Southern in my history. When I was almost seven years old, we moved to Southern California as part of my dad's work with the Shuttle program. And we stayed there until the middle of my sophomore year of high school. I was the daughter of a Southern mother being raised in the climate and culture of Southern California.

Which led to many clashes.

My mother's Mississippi upbringing was rich in manners, gentility, amazing fried chicken, and an Americana small-town setting. It's a gorgeous thing to look back at the pictures from my mother's teen years. Formal dresses with billowing skirts cinched at her tiny waist. A string of pearls at her neck. Day dresses with perfectly pressed seams, satin bow tied neatly. Long white gloves. Hair coiffed and shining, figure slim, shoes the perfect complement to the outfit. The black-and-white photos capturing her as a member of the Homecoming Court and as a cheerleader and at formal dances—well, they're the stuff of Grace Kelly couture dreams. My mother is an only child, and my grandmother poured everything into her only daughter. While my grandparents weren't wealthy, they did provide a favored childhood for my mother. My mom talks about her own mother staying up all night to finish sewing a dress or foregoing new shoes for herself so she could purchase a pair for my mom.

My mother's parents loved her deeply, trained her impeccably, and taught her to care seriously about the opinions of others. In that era and in that environment, people cared deeply about social rules and uniformity and fitting in.

Fast forward almost thirty years to a suburb outside of Los Angeles where an opinionated adolescent heck-bent on individuality and having her own quirky sense of style was passionately trying to carve her own path.

That would be me—daughter of the etiquette-trained, shoes-dyed-to-match-the-dress Southern mom.

I wanted to wear open-toed, white strappy sandals with heels . . . to school . . . after Labor Day. In the California autumn heat, I thought it was no big deal to leave the house in white shorts, but my mom saw it as the end of well-mannered society as we know it. I wanted to wear V-neck sweaters backwards, and I scalped one of my dad's cardigans from his college days, an olive green number with questionable material integrity, as it looked to have been a favorite with the moths. My eyeliner got deeper and darker, my hair bigger and higher. It was a rough ride for my rules-of-the-fashion-runway mother.

I saw it as self-expression.

She saw it is a direct reflection upon herself.

And so went our dance, me marching back up the stairs, dramatically hostile, to change when an accessory or ensemble was deemed out-of-keeping with what was in-season, timely, modest, or acceptable to her.

After becoming a mom myself, I decided I wouldn't get caught up in the same cycle. I was going to let my children be self-expressive in their fashion choices. I would allow them to experiment and create and dabble, fashion etiquette be hanged.

I hung in pretty well with that approach.

Until one day.

You know, that day we all eventually come to—the day when a thing we never thought would bother us . . . well, it bothers us.

That day happened for me a little after Easter when Madison, eight years old at the time, was getting ready for dance. She was wrestling her way into a leotard while I was packing her siblings into the car to make the crosstown trek to the dance studio. The diaper bag had been stuffed with supplies and the little ones had already started squalling when Madison came trotting out of the house, hair in a sloppy ponytail, pink tights adorning her legs, scuffed ballet slippers on her feet, leotard donned.

With an odd feature.

Her chest seemed to have blossomed into adolescent glory, if you catch my idiomatic drift. There were two conical bumps under the leotard, just below the elasticized neckline, making for a rather geometric décolletage. Madison continued her casual stroll out to the car, ready to roll.

I got behind the wheel and began my chauffeur duties, contemplating Madison's pseudo-plastic surgery silhouette. Being that it was right after Easter, it appeared she had taken a plastic Easter egg, separated it at the seam, and placed half in one side of the leotard and half in the other.

Instant curves.

Of a sort.

My mind bounced in a dozen different directions. Did I dare let her attend dance class with this Easter egg-udder feature going on? What if people laughed at her? What if one of her classmates teased her? What if one of the Easter egg halves fell out mid-pirouette? And what would the other dance moms think of me? How would this reflect on me and my parenting?

Oh.

There it was.

That fear.

The fear that someone would judge me based on my kid, on the way she was presenting herself.

My white-shoes-after-Labor-Day moment.

I let my eyes flicker to the rearview mirror, checking to see if the half-eggs were still intact. Yes, they were. And now we were just a few blocks from the dance school.

We pulled into the parking lot. And I let Madison go in, egg enhancements and all.

Later, her dance teacher and I had a huge laugh over it. But it was an important moment. Madison got to try out an experiment in self-expression. And I got to let the leash of public opinion slip a little from my grasp. Which made it easier the next time something like this happened. And the next. Not that Madison ever repeated the Easter egg trick. But there would be plenty of opportunities in which she—as well as the rest of my kids—chose some type of self-expression that wasn't in keeping with my preferences. Nothing big, just not my preference.

And I learned that people do judge and offer their opinions. I allowed one of the girls to wear plastic princess dress-up shoes to church one day, after having warned her they might not be the best choice as it was cold outside and the shoes didn't fit well. She decided it was worth the risk.

Cold toes and three blisters later, we were leaving Sunday school when an older gentleman stopped me and let me have it for allowing my child to come to church in such inappropriate shoes.

Can't we just give each other a break on stuff like this—the things that are just appearances and have nothing to do with real parenting issues like guiding character and unlocking purpose and inculcating a love for Jesus? The caliber of my motherhood hinged on a shoe choice? I was allowing, in a controlled environment, for my child to experience the consequences of her choices. She learned that plastic princess dress-up shoes aren't the best choice for warmth or comfort. I learned that people will sometimes judge. And voice that judgment strongly.

But guess what? I also learned it can be survived. So what if somebody disagrees with the way I let my kid present herself? It's okay. It's not a true reflection of how my parenting gig is going.

Jesus says, "Stop judging by mere appearances, but instead judge correctly" (John 7:24). It's not the accoutrements that count; it's the character. I'd rather have a kid with a strong sense of confidence and a crazy sense of style, all things considered. It's great if my kids remind people of me, but ultimately, I want my kids to reflect Jesus. And Jesus is a pretty radical person.

Jesus is a true original.

―――――――――

It's not an easy thing, to extricate ourselves and our interpretation of ourselves from the identities and expressions of our children. Sometimes the acoustics of our agenda drown out the singular voices of our kids, a wash of white noise covering the quiet song of a rare soul. When I look into the faces of my children, I do see aspects of my own features. I see glimpses of their daddy's smile. I see flashes of my grandmother's eyes, my grandfather's coloring, my brother's profile. The influence of our family and genetics and experiences is reflected in each child. But even in seeing what is familiar in each of them, it's all combined anew in a way that is completely fresh, completely original.

Our children were never intended to be direct reflections of us—or anyone else. They were never meant to carry the weight of our identity and their own. So let's slip the tangle of us from the threads of them. Let's enjoy where we see the translucent tracing of a previous generation recorded into the time capsule of our kids, but let's never allow it to become the primary feature. Let's let God paint. Let's give Him the freedom to show off. Let's think about John the Baptist's words as he celebrated Jesus coming into the fullness of His purpose: "That's why my cup is running over. This is the assigned moment for him to move into the center, while I slip off to the sidelines" (John 3:30 MSG).

PART 3

TOOLS FOR THE TRADE

Raising an Original Personality Evaluation Summary

LEARNING THE ROPES

Discovering Your Child's Personality Style

*It's been a continuity right from the beginning—
that longing to weave together perceptions, to
affirm that richness of us as human beings
both as performers and audience members.*

Meredith Monk

TIME FOR a pop quiz.

Ready?

Hands on the buzzer?

Here we go.

What do the lie detector machine, Wonder Woman, and the systolic blood pressure test have to do with each other?

Anyone?

Clock's ticking.

Okay, I'll go easy on you.

All of those things came from the fertile, inventive mind of William Marston. A compelling and controversial man, Marston held dual degrees in the Arts and Law from Harvard, along with a PhD in psychology. Early on in his research, he and his wife, Elizabeth, noticed a strong correlation between emotions and blood pressure, so much that he developed a machine that measured changes in blood pressure when someone was telling a lie. That innovation is what we know today as the polygraph machine. Over time, Marston expanded his work to look into further aspects of personality and behavior, to the delight of his adherents and to the angst of his detractors. Two books on his research, *Emotions of Normal People* and *Integrative Psychology*, were published in 1928 and 1931, respectively.

Those books became the foundational research for a personality assessment we still use to this day, which ultimately became known as the DiSC test or assessment, first introduced by an industrial psychologist named Walter Vernon Clarke. The DiSC model identifies four primary personality types. No one is completely one specific personality; we're all a gorgeous amalgam of many facets of each, as no inventory can completely capture all the nuances and complexities of an individual. But tools like the DiSC assessment can be helpful in showing certain tendencies as well as revealing the strengths and challenges of different personality styles.

To help us identify the curious threads within our children and to learn more about what makes each individual child tick, I've created a modified DiSC assessment. Up to this point, we've examined what exactly it means to raise an original, and we've become aware of traps that could make us put our faith in external situations rather than in the Father of all our kids. The next step is to fill our parenting toolboxes with tools to help us understand more deeply the children who have been entrusted to us. Just as a lacemaker skillfully utilizes bobbin and needle and thimble, we have some helpful devices at our disposal to benefit us in discovering the curious threads in each of our children.

Oh, and about William Marston being the creator of the comic book character Wonder Woman? Well, that's not really necessary info for our quest—but it *will* make you look like a champ during a Trivial Pursuit match.

You're welcome.

DOUBLE DUTY

It was a chilly day in January of 2007. I was expecting our seventh baby—a bit of a bonus after thinking for a few years that we were holding at our tribe of six kids. I was halfway through the pregnancy, feeling just a little tired, and, as usual, big as a house. But hey, seventh baby and all. Who wouldn't be big and tired, right?

We decided to have a routine ultrasound and a friend of ours from church, Kelly, just happened to be the ultrasound technician. We stopped by her office with all the kids, excited to see if my hunch that this baby was a boy would hold true.

Kelly's ultrasound room had a big, comfy sectional with a large screen on the wall, perfect so the entire family could comfortably view the ultrasound—a theatrical experience instead of everyone crowding around a tiny monitor. I hoisted my pregnant self up onto the exam table and eased my sore back onto the crackling paper, hiking my maternity blouse up over the mound of my stomach so Kelly could squirt that lovely transponder gel onto my stretchmarked canvas of a belly. The kids fought for preferred seats on the sectional and Michael stood by my side, ready to see this newest edition of Carr.

The squish of cold gel, the smooth roller of the transducer, and the flickering shadows of the womb projected onto the big screen. But before my eyes could adjust to take in the murky image, I heard Kelly gasp.

Michael, who all through our pregnancies could literally not seem to make heads or tails of the ultrasound images, said, "Do I see two? Two heads?"

"Julie!" Kelly laughed. "It's twins!"

At first, I really thought she was playing with us. After all, I had long before earned my mama-to-many badge. Surely I'd know if I had twins on board.

But there they were, up on the supersize screen for all to see. Two little babies, nestled together in my womb. Baby A was Merci, slumbering near the bottom of my uterus with Baby B, Jake, stacked on top and kicking his sister in the face.

As my pregnancy with the twins continued, I was constantly in awe of how differently they seemed to behave in utero. Merci would lazily roll and stretch, slowly moving her limbs and pushing gently against her amniotic confines. She seemed to me a somnolent Persian kitty cat, moving with unhurried, queenly deliberation.

And Jake?

Well.

You know those clear plastic balls you can get for your pet hamster? You stick the hamster in the ball and he runs and runs and careens into the legs of the furniture and occasionally loses bladder control and then runs in a circular raincloud of hamster pee until you catch said plastic ball and try to remember if it's okay to bathe pee-covered hamsters.

You know, that whole thing?

That was Jake.

He liked to hang out up under the right-hand side of my rib-cage, running in his amniotic-sac hamster ball all day and all night. At times it felt like he was doing a gymnastics bar routine off my lowest rib. He squirmed, hiccupped, jumped, flipped, ran in place, and moved, moved, moved. He actually even flipped around during delivery, managing to make his appearance face-up with the umbilical cord draped over his shoulders like the ribbon of an Olympic medal.

Those pre-birth twinkles of personality held true after the twins were born. Merci, outweighing her twin by two pounds, liked for things to be calm. She became quite upset with us when the routine chaos of a ten-person household swirled around her. She wanted our full attention and held us responsible for keeping her entertained and fully supplied in binkies. She was a fluffy, round-eyed, dark-haired miniature diva who liked a predictable pattern. And many of those traits are still with nine-year-old Merci today.

Her hamster of a twin weighed two pounds less. Jake was an alert, busy newborn, always moving his arms and legs, loving social stimulation, scooting across the floor early on, and reveling in bathtime fun. He was joyfully, deeply attached to each and every one of his seven siblings, and kinesthetic to a high degree. All that sunniness, all that social attachment, all that movement, all that easy-going joy and quirkiness still shine today.

It wasn't that I hadn't had a sense of my other kids' personalities when I was pregnant with each of them. It was just that carrying two babies at the same time really drove home the differences and individualities and whimsies and originalities that the Lord builds into people, even if they are conceived at the same time and develop as womb mates. The unique strands of character and personality within Merci and Jake were already holding and evident even before their births. It brings to mind a fascinating piece of Scripture from the book of Romans. Paul talks about the twins Jacob and Esau and how God had a plan for those boys before the first labor pain even hit:

Rebekah's children were conceived at the same time by our father Isaac. Yet, before the twins were born or had done anything good or bad—in order that God's purpose in election might stand: not by works but by him who calls—she was told, "The older will serve the younger."

Romans 9:10–12

Rebekah was a little more on the ball than I was when it came to suspecting something unusual going on with her pregnancy. Genesis 25 records that as her babies tumbled and wrestled within her, she was perceptive enough to go to the Lord and ask Him why she was experiencing so much internal activity. God, through divine ultrasound, so to speak, revealed to her that she was carrying two babies—two nations, actually—and the wrestling of these two babies indicated who each of them would be. Esau was born before Jacob, and sure enough, Jacob was born hanging on to his brother's heel, ready even then to trip Esau up from his firstborn status.

Yes, temperament can be present even in the womb. I was delighted to read our lacemaker Zélie's thoughts about her ninth and last pregnancy. Perhaps Zélie knew from the beginning that there was something special about her lastborn, who would one day be known as Saint Thérèse. She wrote to her sister-in-law, "When I was carrying her I noticed something which never happened with my other children; when I sang she sang with me."[9]

I had the opportunity to interview my amazing friend and colleague Dr. Jimmy Myers on the topic of early evidence of temperament. Dr. Myers is an author and therapist in Austin, Texas, who specializes in family and teen counseling. I asked him, "How early do you, as a psychologist, believe that personality begins to reveal itself? Is it discernible if we are equipped to notice?"

Dr. Myers answered, "Almost from the get-go. Parents can see personality differences in their children from infancy. The trick for parents is to begin adapting their parenting style to that child's personality as early as possible."

Now, don't get me wrong. I'm not saying that people are born preset and can't make changes, can't transform, can't experience growth. Not at all. I'm talking about the incredible gift of original temperament and personality that God places in each individual at the spark of conception. He selects remarkable seeds of soul and fingerprint and disposition and endows each human being with their own mix. Each of us has our own custom blend to manage. Whether or not we choose to place it in God's purpose—that's the crossroads at which each of us will arrive at some point in life's journey.

King David came to that crossroads. He was ambitious. Passionate. Impulsive. Powerful. Creative. Those strong traits could bring him purpose—or perdition. In his affair with the beautiful Bathsheba and his machinations to ensure the death of her husband, Uriah, David exhibited each of those traits in their most negative aspect. When the prophet Nathan confronted David about his murderous infidelity, the king was pierced emotionally and took up his pen to confess before God. He wrote in the fifty-first Psalm—the poem in which he owned up to his deeds—his awareness that he had made poor use of all with which God had gifted him: "Yet you desired faithfulness even in the womb; you taught me wisdom in that secret place" (Psalm 51:6).

Back when I was working on my undergraduate degree in psychology at Abilene Christian University, there was general consensus amongst prominent child development specialists that one's personality was formed by the time they were twelve years old. To assess one's personality before that age was deemed premature. But in the two-and-a-half decades plus since I completed my degree, more extensive study has led researchers to believe that a child's personality is quite observable at a much younger age. At first, researchers dropped the personality age set to seven, and now, today's experts believe children preschool age and younger show strong strands of personality that are still very much in evidence when they become adults.

The Journal of Personality, in Volume 76 of the February 2008 edition, and reported by NBC News, revealed the results of a study that had gone on for nineteen years. Researchers asked teachers to evaluate traits of children in their classrooms between the ages of four and six. The study specifically looked at kids who tended to be shy and kids who tended to be more aggressive. As the children in the study grew and matured over the next two decades, researchers found that their tendencies toward shyness or aggression stayed with them as they entered the adult world of higher education, relationships, and employment. The researchers were struck by how consistently traits evident in early childhood stayed with these kids into their adult lives.[10]

A 2003 article from *The Journal of Personality* takes that age even younger, as researchers evaluated numerous three-year-olds on twenty-two different behavior traits and then followed up until the subjects were twenty-six. In a nutshell? The three-year-old kid was still highly recognizable in the personality of the twenty-six-year-old adult. The study's author, psychology professor Avshalom Caspi, wrote about the importance of the findings:

> If early emerging behavioral differences did not predict outcomes, behavioral scientists, parents, and teachers could safely ignore such individual differences. However, because such differences do shape the course of development, information about these individual differences can be harnessed to design parent-trained programs and school-based interventions to improve children's development.[11]

Now, before you throw your hands up and think, "Well, fantastic! This would've been helpful information back when my kid was a toddler, but now we're in the wilds of teenagehood. Does that mean original-raising game over?" the short answer is *no*. There is tremendous value, no matter what age our child is, in continuing to be thread seekers and in continuing to invest in discovering the contours of our child's heart.

If your child is older, you have an unexpected gift. I've discovered that with my kids who are older, there is an absolute fascination on their part to participate in all manner of personality assessment. As humans, we seem to be wired for and enthralled by self-discovery. In fact, if you're having a difficult time communicating with your teen, talking through personality styles together could be that bridge you need.

At this point, it's time to complete the ROPES—or Raising an Original Personality Evaluation Summary—assessment. We're going to build a personality profile for each of the kids in your life—a tangible original owner's manual, if you will, that will help bring outline and form to that mystery of your child's personality. Because in order to raise an original, you've got to have an understanding of just who that person is.

After you've completed the ROPES assessment, we're going to explore what motivates and challenges that particular personality as well as the best ways to influence, discipline, and help guide those curious threads. And after you've worked through this assessment for each of your children, I want to encourage you to take it for yourself. It's critical to understand our own personalities and temperaments when it comes to the way we parent and how we interact with our kids.

Go ahead and brew a pot of coffee or a cup of tea, grab your favorite pen and perhaps a journal or some extra paper (if you'll be assessing multiple children), and prayerfully begin this personality assessment. Remember, the information you discover about your kids will be critical to learning who they are and raising them as the originals God created them to be. And invite your teens to join you in discerning their unique temperament. Chances are, they'll love the opportunity to discover more about who they are.

LEARNING THE ROPES

As we begin to seek threads of personality in our children, let's start with a few simple observations. If you carried your child through pregnancy, what do you remember thinking about her? Were there things that you noticed? Did your yet-to-be-born baby seem to have a little routine, sleeping at certain times of the day and active at others? In utero, was he quiet, strong, delicate, or busy? Jot down three words that best characterize what you noticed most about your child up to birth. For example, my youngest child, Jake—that little hamster-in-the-ball kiddo—brings to mind three words: Active. Busy. Alert. For Merci, his twin, I wrote down three different words: Deliberate. Scheduled. Restive. Other options you might consider: Strong. Delicate. Predictable. Calm. Serene. Attached. Sweet.

Now, if you really didn't seem to notice many specifics during the pregnancy or if that's not information you have access to because God built your family through adoption or fostering, or if you're reading this book as a caregiver, teacher, or extended family member invested in the life of a child, no worries. We've still got plenty of options for discovering those threads of personality. The above exercise simply helps us begin to flex and strengthen our "noticing" muscles.

And speaking of noticing, what were the first things you noticed about your child as a little baby? What stands out to you most when you look back on those early days? Was your baby colicky or laid-back? An early bird or a night owl? Or maybe an always-awake, shrieking, circling pterodactyl!

In my world, my third child and oldest son, Justus, was very attached to me as a small child. In fact, he still—in all his young adult, six-foot-plus glory, declares unabashedly that he is a "Mama's boy." You can imagine how much I hate that. Not.

Justus was fascinated by his older sisters and always incredibly aware of the people around him. A sensitive baby and toddler, he'd startle at loud noises and weepily respond to anyone who tried to play peekaboo with him. Yes, peekaboo freaked him out. He also seemed to have ears like a bat and was early on trying to emulate speech and sounds. In this phase of his childhood, I would have described him as Attached, People-Oriented, Kinesthetically Sensitive, Aware, and (sorry, Justus) High Maintenance.

Now it's your turn. What words and phrases come to mind when you think about your child from birth to age two? Easygoing? Happy? Touchy? Eager? Easily frustrated? Make sure you include both the delightful and challenging aspects of this season. Note your observations. And feel free to pull out videos and pictures of this time in your child's life. Sometimes, the sleep-deprived hazy depths of life with a young baby can make recall of these days a challenge. I'm always amazed at what memories come flooding back when I take advantage of the time machine we call photography.

A child begins to assert his individuality even more noticeably as he develops language and becomes steadier on his feet. At this age, what was your child like? Eager to communicate? More shy? Fearless when he became more mobile, attempting to scale any obstacle? Or happy to stay put in a room with you?

Write down some of the descriptions and observations you have of your child through toddlerhood.

Now, recopy all the descriptive words and observations you recalled from your child's pre-birth, baby, and toddler years.

Before we move on to the next step, don't get too caught up in your choices. Just as we can have many "sides" to our personalities, so can our kids. What we're seeking here is the most dominant threads. So go with the choice that best describes what your child would most often do. If your child is past this age, still answer the following questions as closely as possible to how you remember them at that age. The more information we can gather, the more high-definition a picture we can ultimately see.

AGES TWO TO SIX

When asked to pick up a toy or participate in a simple, age-appropriate chore, your child . . .

1. immediately offers an alternate option that she is certain is better.
2. first tells you something that is completely unrelated.
3. seems to enjoy working alongside you and prefers to have you there.

4. dives in and is soon ready for the next item on the list.

In a social setting with kids of similar age, your child . . .

1. leads the pack, so to speak. Other kids seem to quickly allow him to direct the game and dictate how they're going to play.

E 2. is the first one on the playground to strike up a conversation and loves to act goofy, inspiring the laughter and attention of others.

C JA 3. prefers to have playdates with just a couple of friends instead of being part of a bigger group.

4. becomes very concerned when her playmates aren't playing the game "right" or aren't following the rules.

When you receive feedback about your child from preschool teachers, Sunday school teachers, babysitters, other parents, and extended family, your child is most commonly described as . . .

1. confident and strong-willed.

J E A 2. personable and happy.

3. cooperative and calm.

C 4. careful and thoughtful.

Your child's area of challenge that you're most likely to be working on or commenting on is . . .

J 1. being bossy.

E A 2. having a lack of focus and follow-through, such as getting sidetracked when going to put away his shoes.

3. worrying too much about what others might think or how others might feel.

C

4. struggling with making the "right" choice and not wanting to be wrong.

In the proverbial question "Is the glass half full or half empty?" your child would most likely respond . . .

1. "I'll ask the questions here."
2. "Half full and will probably be overflowing soon!"
3. "What would make you the happiest, half full or half empty?"
4. "Clearly, half empty."

When playing with a set of blocks or Legos, your child . . .

1. builds something quickly, maybe a little lopsided, but still, don't help me.
2. has the pieces talk to each other and ends up conducting an entire soap opera.
3. really, really, really would prefer you build with him.
4. deliberately and carefully builds and if a blueprint manual is available, all the better.

In a large group setting, your child . . .

1. wants to lead the crowd.
2. wants to entertain the crowd.
3. wants to be part of the crowd, but preferably not a big crowd.
4. thinks crowds are overrated and doesn't mind going it alone.

In this next section, we'll get a little more specific, as the age range here focuses on seven and older. Go through this inventory

first by yourself on behalf of your child. Then, go back and have
your child respond to each of the questions. I've done a variety
of personality profiles with my kids through the years, and I've
found that kids have pretty good insight about themselves. With
some of my kids, we agreed answer for answer. With others, I
learned so much from listening to their responses that outward
behavior trends covered the inner dialog of their hearts. And a
word of caution: Take care not to argue with your kids about their
answers. This is not about right or wrong. It's about discovery.

AGES SEVEN AND UP

What word best describes you? Of course, you can be all these
things—and you probably are—but what word really stands out
to you?

1. Bold
2. Happy
3. Nice
4. Smart

What do you like most about your best friend?

1. She/he thinks I'm really smart.
2. We laugh a lot and have a good time together. She/he
   thinks I'm funny.
3. I just like having someone to do things with. She's/he's
   really, really nice.
4. We like the same things and we like to do them the
   same way.

I would prefer to . . .

1. play (and hopefully win) a game.
2. laugh or watch a funny movie and act it out.
3. help someone.
4. put together a puzzle or make a craft.

Of these four things, the one that makes me the most uncomfortable is . . .

1. someone cheating and taking my spot.
2. other kids not liking me or being left out.
3. having somebody be mad at me.
4. making a mistake or not knowing the answer to a question.

For the next two questions, you may like most of the things listed. But pick your most favorite thing.

I like . . .

1. to lead a project or adventure.
2. to go to parties.
3. to listen to stories.
4. to organize things (my room, my desk, my locker).

I also like . . .

1. doing lots of things at once.
2. making new friends.
3. listening to my friends.
4. getting my schoolwork right.

I feel happiest when . . .

1. I nail the perfect move in dance class or when I score in my game.
2. I'm having a great time with my friends. *C*
3. something goes just the way I'd hoped.
4. I get an answer right.

I really don't like it when . . .

1. someone won't do what I say. *C*
2. people aren't laughing at my jokes or listening to me.
3. someone changes plans at the last minute.
4. someone tells me I'm wrong.

This next section is for individuals of all ages. If you're assessing teens or tweens, make sure they've also provided you with answers for the inventory in the previous sections. Some terms are seemingly more positive and some are seen as a bit of a challenge. Have your teen or tween identify three positive attributes they believe fit their personality and three attributes that describe some of the challenges in their personality. If your child is between toddlerhood and age six, select three descriptors from the box on the left and two descriptors from the box on the right.

Choose three descriptors from this box:	If your child is seven or older, choose three descriptors from this box. If your child is six or younger, choose two descriptors.		
Compliant	Argumentative *E*		
Consistent *Ju*	Avoids Confrontation		
Creative *A E Ja*	Controlling		
Decisive	Critical *C Ja*		
Enthusiastic *A Ju*	Dislikes Change *E Ju*		
Finisher *Ju C*	Emotional *A*		
Forgiving	Hogs the Spotlight *A*		
Helpful *A C*	Impulsive *A*		
Inspiring	Messy		
Logical *Ja*	Overly Cautious *C*		
Opinionated	Perfectionistic *Ju C Ja*		
Outgoing *E*	Pushy *Ju*		
Precise	Reserved		
Risk Taker *E*	Selfish		
Thorough *C Ja*	Stubborn *E Ja*		
Understanding	Worried		

So what do all these answers and adjectives mean? Let's stitch it all together.

If you were able to provide a few adjectives from your child's pre-birth through toddler years, list those again in this box. These terms won't be scored, but they do give you insight about your child's temperament.

Now, take a look at the section or sections you completed for ages two to six and also for ages seven and up. Record the answers you marked in Box 1 and Box 2 below. For example, if three of your answers in the ages two-to-six section were 1's, and if four of your answers in the seven-and-up sections were also 1's, then your child would have a total of seven 1's in the box labeled "Total Answers #1."

Box 1

Total #1 answers	Total #2 answers	Total #3 answers	Total #4 answers
A E Jv 1 6 2	A E Jv 10 7 4	A E4Jv 2 2 9	A E Jv 2 0 0

Ja 2 C3 C 1   Ja 3 C7 Ja3 C4

Next, let's review the descriptor selections you made. Go back to that section, and circle your answers below.

Box 2

Decisive	Inspiring	Helpful *A C*	Logical *Ja*
Risk Taker *E*	Outgoing *E*	Understanding	Precise
Pushy *Jv*	Emotional *A*	Reserved	Compliant
Argumentative *E*	Impulsive *A*	Worried	Thorough *Ja C*
Opinionated	Enthusiastic *AJv*	Consistent *Jv*	Perfectionist *JgC*
Finisher *C Jv*	Creative *A E J*	Forgiving	Stubborn *E Ja*
Controlling *Ja*	Messy	Dislikes Change *JE*	Overly Cautious *C*
Selfish	Hogs the Spotlight *A*	Avoids Confrontation	Critical *Ja C*
Totals: *E C J* 8	*A E* 15 9	*A C E* 3 1 3	*Ja C E* 5 4 1

Now, add the totals from Box 1 to the totals from Box 2, going straight down the column. For example, if you had three #1 answers and circled two of the adjectives from the column directly below it (the column with Decisive, Risk Taker, Argumentative, etc.), then you would have a total of five in that column.

Box 3

Total of this column	Total of this column	Total of this column	Total of this column
A E Jv 1 8	*A E Jv* 15 9	*A E Jv* 3 3	*A E Jv* 2 1

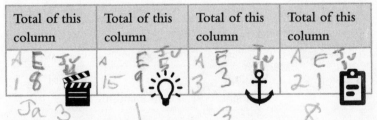

Ja 3   1   3   8

At this point, there should be one column that has a higher number of answers than the others.

BY WAY OF EXAMPLE

Let's look at the following example of scoring the inventory. Let's say we did this inventory for "John Smith" and here's how the scoring turned out:

Raising an Original Personality Evaluation Summary (ROPES) for John Smith:

Box 1

Total #1 answers	Total #2 answers	Total #3 answers	Total #4 answers
7	3	1	4

Box 2

Decisive	Inspiring	Helpful	Logical
Risk Taker	Outgoing	Understanding	Precise
Pushy	Emotional	Reserved	Compliant
Argumentative	Impulsive	Worried	Thorough
Opinionated	Enthusiastic	Consistent	Perfectionist
Finisher	Creative	Forgiving	Stubborn
Controlling	Messy	Dislikes Change	Overly Cautious
Selfish	Hogs the Spotlight	Avoids Confrontation	Critical
Totals: 3	1		2

Box 3 (totals of Box 1 and Box 2)

Total of this column	Total of this column	Total of this column	Total of this column
Box 1 + Box 2 = 10	Box 1 + Box 2 = 4	Box 1 + Box 2 = 1	Box 1 + Box 2 = 6
10 🎬	4 💡	1 ⚓	6 📋

So for our "John Smith," his highest total is 10 in the movie clapboard column. (We'll get to those symbols in a bit.) His second highest total is 6 in the clipboard column. The observations you made about his pre-birth through toddler years are also valuable, so keep those in mind as we talk through the temperaments.

Because of the way I developed this assessment, one column will usually come out with a higher total than the rest. That column is your child's most dominant temperament. You may have two columns that are very close or that even tie. That's where the adjectives you used to describe your child in his younger years will help. As you look over the temperament descriptions in the next chapter, those earlier adjectives will help you hone in on which temperament is the most dominant.

What about those answers your child gave you? Remember, you'll have two sets of answers if you went through the assessment with your child and they answered for themselves. Most often, even if you have a couple different answers to the questions, you'll probably arrive at the same dominant personality style. But sometimes the way a parent sees a child and the way a child sees herself can result in two different personality styles. Nobody has messed up the assessment. This is actually fantastic information, particularly if you've really struggled to understand your child.

As we take a deeper look at the four dominant personalities in the following chapter, you'll have additional insight to help you understand your child.

And let's keep one more thing in mind as we learn how to wield this tool of discovery: This assessment isn't meant to be diagnostic. Rather, it's meant to be directional.

What we're seeking here are clues and a heading for raising our originals. No child will fall squarely and completely within one temperament. That's part of the beauty. Every one of us is a gorgeous compilation of contradictions and ironies. And that's just fine. Enjoy seeing all the nuances, exploring all the places where your kid's personality goes off-road. We're in pioneer country here, unmapped land. Let this assessment help you see the major landmarks, and then look to your child to fill in the details.

Let's put pencil to paper once again. Circle which symbol came in first when you took the assessment for your child:

Which one came in second?

If your child is old enough to take the assessment for herself, which symbols came in first and second for them? Did your conclusions match? What do you think about that?

You also took the ROPES for yourself. What came in as your dominant personality thread? What came in second?

We'll be getting into far more detail in the next chapter, but for now, here's an overview about each personality style and the symbol associated with it.

The Director	The Inspirer
With a love for directing all the action, the Director is decisive and loves to lead people.	The Inspirer temperament lights up the room and always has an idea for having some fun.
The Steadfast	The Curator
An anchor of stability and steadiness, the Steadfast is a great support to friends and a devoted listener.	Conscientious and precise, the Curator loves to tackle a project with thoroughness and a good checklist.

By way of helping us understand these four personality styles even further, take a look at the following chart that shows how the Director, the Inspirer, the Steadfast, and the Curator fall within some familiar lines.

People Oriented   Task Oriented

Extroverted   Introverted

Now that you have a little familiarity with the four temperaments we're going to be exploring, let's head into the next chapter and really get into the specifics of what makes your child truly an original.

CHAPTER 8

PRACTICING THE ROPES

Nurturing Your Child's Original Style

*At the heart of personality is the need
to feel a sense of being lovable without
having to qualify for that acceptance.*

Paul Tournier

THERE'S AN ITEM in my dresser drawer that I simply love. It might not be something anyone else would wear. It might not attract the eyes of the busy shopper. It certainly would not say to another person what it says to me. Yep. You read that right. I have something in my dresser drawer that talks to me.

In a sense.

A few years ago, my friend Denise and her husband traveled to Italy for their twenty-fifth anniversary. They took in all the sights and sampled the amazing food as they regenerated and reconnected.

And somewhere in all of that, Denise thought of me.

They were in Venice, that incredible sinking city of canals and art and glass. Somewhere, in a little shop, sat an item that caught

Denise's eye and reminded her of me. She bought it and brought it home to Texas.

When I opened Denise's present, I felt known.

Seen.

Understood.

It's a ring—huge, vibrant, green—made of hand-blown glass. Its dome is crafted into a large square and the band is also glass, welded through the rendering of sand and heat. Inside the glass is a crackle of gold, fissures of sparkle and darkness marking the verdant depths. It fits on my right hand perfectly. It fits *me* perfectly.

This ring talking to me—how does it do that? Well, it tells me that Denise knows me, knows what captures my eye and my imagination. It tells me she remembers that my irises are really and truly green, even though a lot of people think they're brown. It tells me she remembers that art and beauty and Italy and the unusual all speak to me.

And as big and audacious an accessory as this ring is, it is made of . . . glass. Denise knows this about me. She sees what others might miss. Yes, I can be the loudest laugh at the party and the biggest storyteller and the chattiest vision caster. But, I have my own fragile places and tender spots, places that I could shatter and splinter.

What could say that better than a gorgeous piece of green Venetian glass fitted around my finger? It's not just about a piece of jewelry. It's about what that piece of jewelry represents. And it's about my friendship with Denise.

I'm known.

I'm seen.

I'm understood.

Which makes me feel loved.

There's an interesting name in the Bible. *Beer Lahai Roi.* It was given to God. Yes, someone gave a nickname to God. The woman who gave this name felt utterly unknown and unseen. Her name was Hagar, and she was the servant girl of Sarah.

You remember Sarah, right? Her challenges with infertility made her turn to desperate measures. She had her husband, Abraham, sleep with Hagar in order to impregnate her. Sarah thought this would lead to a pseudo-surrogacy, that maybe this would be the way to finally bring a child into her arms and her home. But Sarah underestimated how deep the stab of jealously would go when Hagar became pregnant. Hagar resented her boss. Sarah, in turn, made life unbearable for Hagar. And so Hagar took off.

Hagar had traveled deep into the countryside when an angel found her. The angel asked where she was going, and she told him she was running away. He told her to return to Abraham and Sarah and gave her some details about the baby she was carrying and the legacy she would have. He also told her the Lord knew of her situation and of the challenges she faced.

Hagar was not alone.

She was not unseen by God.

And so Hagar gave God a name. *Beer Lahai Roi*. It means, "You are the God who sees me." How powerful is that—to know you are seen, you are known, you are deeply understood by God, your Parent? As parents to our own kids, we can help them feel seen, heard, and understood—a phenomenal gift that nourishes a healthy identity in Christ.

That's the kind of opportunity we have before us, now that we've worked through identifying threads in our kids. We have this brilliant juncture in which to demonstrate to our own original children that they are known, understood, seen, and embraced for exactly who they are—what makes them tick, what makes them bold, what makes them scared, what touches them, what defines them. When we show someone we "get" them, that speaks love.

So while we've been answering questions and tallying up answers and figuring out which personality style fits our kid, we've also been equipping ourselves with some tools for demonstrating love to that child.

It's now time to take the information we gathered in the ROPES assessment and put it into practice. If you haven't yet completed the assessment, now is the time! Turn back to the previous chapter and fill it in, then come right back here and we'll continue on this journey.

THE FOUR PERSONALITY STYLES AND THEIR BLENDS

When you completed the assessment, you identified a primary personality trait, the one that had the most answers within its category. But you also identified a secondary trait as well.

We're going to unpack the primary trait first, and then we'll take a look at the secondary trait. The combination of the two will give us even more information about your child's strengths and challenges.

THE DIRECTOR

Some personality types are a bit mysterious. They're not always easy to spot or recognize, their contours somewhat gauzy and vague.

And then there are the personality types that aren't mysterious at all.

The Director is a prime example of the easy-to-spot variety.

Task-oriented, bold, decisive, opinionated, and strong, the Director likes to be in charge. The Director will stand up for what she wants and will rally the troops to get a project completed. Of our eight kids, three are Directors. *Three.* Talk about a lot of cooks in the kitchen. Sheesh!

When our oldest daughter, Madison, was about fifteen years old, she was at her friend's Sweet Sixteen celebration with some other teens and noticed an older guy in his early twenties hanging around the party. There were chaperones at the event, but they were deep in conversation with each other. Madison kept an eye on the older guy, observing that he seemed a bit furtive. As she edged closer to where he was interacting with the teens, she observed him surreptitiously pouring vodka into their sodas, sometimes with their enthusiastic, clandestine permission, sometimes without. Madison made sure to witness a few of these drink spikes before she headed off to find a chaperone. She then hauled the chaperone over to Vodka Guy and directly informed the chaperone what was going on.

Understand, Madison is one of my most petite daughters. She's a diminutive brunette with green eyes who stands several inches shorter than her mama. But her directness gives her an illusion of height. Vodka Guy, on the other hand, towered over both Madison and the chaperone. As Madison concluded her accusations of his illegal bartending, Vodka Guy scoffed and said, "Little girl, you don't know what you're talking about." Madison raised up on her petite feet, pointed her slim finger right at him, tossed her hair over her shoulder, and declared, "You, sir, are a liar!"

That would be the Director personality in her full glory.

Very concerned with fair and unfair, Directors don't mind shaking up the present state of affairs to get to a better outcome.

AGES AND STAGES

What you might notice first if you've got a Director in the house is a baby or toddler who actively engages people. This child is bold and adventurous. This is a kid who—if no one else is available—will pull eggs out of the fridge and climb on top of the cabinet to reach a bowl so she can start making a cake because that's what she wants to do, no matter that she's three years old and can't read a recipe. In my experience, the leadership component of the Director shows up early. This is the kid who gets everyone lined up and organized to go out for preschool recess. This is the kid who isn't afraid to ask the Sunday school teacher why things have to be done a certain way. This is the kid who delights in organizing a family activity and assigns everyone a task. This is the kid who loves to give a good challenge and gets just as much pleasure in taking one.

Directors love to win, which means they hate to lose. Game night at our house—with three Directors in the group and several others who have Director as their strong secondary personality trait—can turn into a crazy, combative event, full of hollering and positioning and laughing and protesting. In our family dynamic, if we need all hands on deck for a project or event, I can turn to one of my Directors, imbue them with my parental authority, and turn them loose. They're more than happy to barrel through the protesting and groaning of their siblings to reach the final goal.

KNOTS AND NOTS

As with each of the personality types we'll be exploring, there are both strengths and challenges to going through life as a Director. In keeping with the idea that we're seeking the curious threads in our kids, I like to think of these as *Knots*—places of strength in the weaving—and *Nots*—areas that require extra guidance and coaching.

With the Director, the obvious Knots are boldness, candor, a can-do spirit, an ability to make quick and firm decisions, and an innate ability to organize people into effective teams. Whether it's enlisting the neighborhood kids in a game of hide-and-seek or arranging a protest against an unfair school policy, the Director can use his strengths to command change. But he also has some Nots that he needs to be aware of as he interacts with others. Because of his drive and appetite for achievement, he can struggle with listening to others and equally valuing their thoughts and ideas as highly as his own. Because he is so focused on outcomes, he can forget that people should come before projects. And because others will naturally be drawn to him, he'll need to work to make sure he's not always center stage. He's going to need your coaching to remember that people are not commodities to be used but instead relationships to be cultivated.

Proverbs 28 is a fantastic chapter that explains the potential of bold leadership as well as the pitfalls of using people for your own means. It's an insightful resource for talking your Director through her God-given originality and the ways in which she can use it well.

STILL AN ORIGINAL

I mentioned earlier that I have three kids with Director as their primary personality type. But here's something I love that God does, even in the template of a discernible personality style. My second daughter, McKenna, also presents as a Director—and she and Madison are extremely different people. Yes, both are bold. Both are organized. Both are activators within their communities. But the expression of those Director traits through the uniqueness of each of my daughters creates a new blend. And they each present with a secondary personality style that supplements and singularizes their individuality.

THE BLENDS

DI—If your child came up with D as his first trait and I as his second, you've got what I call the Directionally Inspired. This combination is hugely driven, curious, and project-motivated. The I part of this combination spectacularly and persuasively enhances the strong leadership component of the D. If your child has this blend, they may already dream of running the free world, and they'll have the charm and people-savvy to gain momentum.

DS—If your child came up with D as her first trait and S as her second, you can think of her as Directionally Steadfast. The calmness and steadiness of the S personality gives a stabilizing effect to the more passionate D. The drive of the D and the loyalty of the S combine to create a personality with all kinds of perseverance and staying power when it comes to accomplishing big tasks and endeavors.

DC—If your child came up with D as his first trait and C as his second, you've got a powerhouse in your home. I call this personality the Directed Curator. It's a potent combination. All the focus and detail-orientation of the C personality infuses the ambition of the D. These are the folks who can plow through objections and hurdles and often prefer to work alone since they know they'll get it right. They'll need your guidance to not veer into being a stubborn lone wolf who might just take over the world.

THE INSPIRER

I've got three of these too. The Inspirer.

The Inspirer has some characteristics similar to the Director, but this personality type takes a slightly different course. The Inspirer inspires (surprise!) others to participate in life with him, joining him in whatever new idea has caught his eye and sounds like fun. Gifted at encouraging and engaging, the Inspirer is people-oriented over task-oriented. The Inspirer also has a thriving sense of humor, and it's that humor which makes him so attractive to others. Fairly laid-back, Inspirers don't get too riled up about details. Through charm and good nature, the Inspirer is very influential amongst his peers, not because he's forceful but instead because he's just plain fun.

Creative problem solving—often without fully thinking through the consequences—is another hallmark of the Inspirer. When my oldest son, Justus—an Inspirer—was around five years old, we allowed the kids to get three fish, which we housed in an aquarium in the kids' bathroom. The three fish were all a little different from each other. Madison chose a standard goldfish and named her Goldie, while McKenna selected her Angel, a beautiful white veiltail goldfish, its gossamer tail and fins as dramatic and delicate as the train of a bridal gown. Justus chose a little guy who looked like a calico kitten, in a fish kind of way, with scaly splotches of brown, white, and orange. Inexplicably, he named his fish Basketball. We also added a suckerfish for good measure, hoping to keep the tank a bit cleaner.

One day I ventured into the kids' bathroom to put away some clean towels. Turning to check on the aquarium, I discovered to my surprise that one of the goldfish had disappeared. McKenna's dramatic veil-tailed Angel was missing. I peered into the aquarium from various angles, trying to see if she was perhaps hiding behind the sunken treasure chest decoration. No Angel.

I then glanced over at the sink, where I noticed the stopper had been removed. I glimpsed what looked like a wet piece of toilet paper draped along the depths of the basin, which, upon closer look, was actually a gasping Angel wedged in the drain. I'm still not completely sure how I fished that fish out of the sink, but somehow I managed it in one of those supermom triage kind of moments. Then I hollered for the kids to come upstairs. After a time of questioning, the chain of events was revealed. Justus, the Inspirer, had noticed that the aquarium was getting a bit dingy, and since Angel had the lightest colored scales, he'd decided to give her a bath. In the sink. With soap. Creative problem solving? Yes. Considering the consequences? Uh . . . no. Believe it or not, Angel survived, albeit her delicate tail in tatters and her demeanor a bit more paranoid. And she burped soap bubbles for a while.

AGES AND STAGES

The Inspirer loves to entertain, even pre-language. Our daughter Journey is an Inspirer and while still a tiny toddler, she would prompt an entire restaurant to sing the ABCs with her, most of her phonetics garbled but her melody enthusiastic. The Inspirer loves to laugh and to make others laugh. You may notice a sense of wit that seems advanced for her age. Early and strong verbal communication skills have been evident in two of my Inspirers. My third Inspirer—our youngest child, Jake—was late on verbal skills but adept in communicating through raw charm, inspiring his nickname, Little Charmer.

Our kids who are Inspirers expressed strong emotions early

on—both joy and sadness. They just feel the *feels* so much. When they're happy, nobody is happier. When they're feeling down, it's a low down. Life is just a vibrant, intense, generally enjoyable enterprise for them. The Inspirer is also one who expresses strong physical affection, both in the giving and in the need to receive.

KNOTS AND NOTS

When it comes to inspiring and leading others, in expanding vision and in motivating through encouragement, the Inspirer is all that. It's a powerful Knot in the personality thread. The Not? All that connection and gourmet approach to life also puts the Inspirer at risk of focusing too much on people-pleasing and vigorously fearing rejection. The Inspirer will need your coaching to not to make pleasing and entertaining the crowd her highest aim.

Another strong Knot for the Inspirer is a zeal for taking on new challenges along with a willingness to throw himself into fresh experiences. The accompanying Not is a lack of attention to detail and a tendency to avoid the more mundane tasks of life. Finally, because the Inspirer lives so comfortably in the warmth of the spotlight—another Knot—you'll need to teach him to allow others to have the attention sometimes.

Turn to Proverbs 19 for a great discussion about wisdom, diligence, and good decision-making tips especially for Inspirers.

THE BLENDS

ID—If your child came up with I first and then D, she is Inspirationally Directed. She still enjoys her ability to inspire others, but with the infusion of D traits, she can inspire people to engage more specific causes. The ID usually comes off as highly energetic and somewhat distracted as her mind races through ideas and inspiration, along with connecting with the people around her.

IS—If your child came up with I first and then S, you have the delight of having someone in your home who is Inspirationally Steadfast. This personality blend loves people, is a trusted counselor to his friends, and thrives in serving others. He can toggle seamlessly between the limelight and the backstage. People always come before pursuits, which means that chores can get sidelined if a friend in need shows up. This blend tends to get along well with all sorts of people. My sixth child, Journey, has this blend in almost equal proportions, and it never ceases to amaze me how she gets along with and enjoys friends with wildly different personalities.

IC—If your child came up with I first and then C, you've got an Inspired Curator. This is someone who is persuasive but also attentive to details. The IC has the ability to communicate instruction well—because of her people skills, she knows how to interact comfortably, but she can also supply needed particulars to equip others for the job at hand. She does love to win and can be unwilling to explore new options since she doesn't want to risk messing up.

THE STEADFAST

Dependable. Conscientious. Steady. Loyal. That's the Steadfast. I so appreciate the Steadfasts in my life. They are kind, friendly, and consistent. They're the kind of people who show up, do the job, rarely complain, and leave with a smile. No drama, no fuss. We've got one kid, Jairus, who—by just one point on the assessment— shows the Steadfast as his dominant personality style. The Steadfast is easygoing, kind, and likes working alongside others. They're the affable workhorses of the world, happy to come alongside and shovel the detritus of the enthusiastic vision casters. They're the ones who take the task to the end.

Jairus, our fifth child, showed some of his Steadfast characteristics early. When he was only about a year old, we went to visit my parents in Utah. My brothers and their families joined us for a raucous, laughter-filled reunion. One morning, I got up early and found Jairus awake as well. I went downstairs with him and deposited him in the highchair. My brothers and my mom had also made their way to the kitchen, and in their chatting hadn't realized that Jairus was sitting there, highchair angled so he had a view of everyone. Everyone was laughing and talking—hootin' and hollerin' as we Southerners would call it—bringing a boisterous volume level to an otherwise quiet morning. My brother Rob happened to glance over to where Jairus sat. Light brown baby hair standing straight up and wide green eyes happily taking in the scene, Jairus hadn't made a sound, hadn't demanded any attention. He just basked in observing, content as could be.

AGES AND STAGES

The Steadfast as a baby or toddler is a content little person, a sea of calm amongst his Whirling Dervish preschool classmates . . . as long as he knows you're around. Steadfasts don't need to have a crowd, but they do like *their* people. That one-on-one relationship with a parent is of particular importance in the early ages, as Steadfasts are woven for deep connection. A Steadfast, even while still very young, is most happy simply being around the individuals who are most familiar to him. If you add a new baby to the family while your Steadfast is still in the toddler phase, pay particular attention to keeping that toddler snuggled up close and part of the new baby experience. Because a Steadfast so values relationship, a new member added to the family will be a sweet thing for him, but he needs to know that his connection with you remains strong and solid.

Because Steadfasts don't like to rock the boat, it's crucial to listen with your heart when it comes to being aware of what might be tumbling around in the thought life of a Steadfast. These are the kids who you don't always realize have been left out, unacknowledged, or manipulated by a friend with a stronger streak of determination. Steadfasts can exemplify the adage "Still waters run deep," and you'll want to ask leading questions and then listen well. Because my Steadfast, Jairus, often preferred not to rock the boat, I would sometimes discover that even though externally all seemed fine, a situation with a playmate or worry about a circumstance would have been poking at his heart for weeks and weeks before I even knew about it. Sometimes a Steadfast will need your "permission" to speak up and call something or someone out.

KNOTS AND NOTS

The great strength of the Steadfast is, of course, that Knot of steadiness, that calm demeanor. Another Knot is his capacity for friendship. The Steadfast's genuine kindness and consideration are the stuff of committed and healthy relationships. But all that steadiness finds change extremely difficult—a Not he'll need help navigating through. Because feeling secure is of such high value to the Steadfast, any circumstances that feel wobbly and precarious are difficult for him. He'll need your encouragement to try new things, to make modifications, to step out of his comfort zone.

Psalm 112 is a great piece of Scripture to review with your Steadfast. It shows the powerful interplay of a steadfast heart that learns to trust God in challenge and in change.

THE BLENDS

SD—If your child came up with S first and then D, he's a Steadfast Director. He leads small groups of people well and can capably complete tasks with a small team. The Steadfast calm of his demeanor can help temper the more intense disposition of the D. This blend can have a wealth of endurance.

SI—If your child shows S as her primary type and I as her secondary, welcome to the Steadfast Inspirer. That collision of the two types that are both highly people-oriented makes for a personality that usually enjoys many friendships. This blend has a high capacity to enjoy a wide variety of people, with an easy pliancy and a broad aptitude for forgiveness. This blend is also gifted at knowing how to include everyone, even those who might typically stand outside the circle.

SC—The SC blend is the Steadfast Curator. If your child presents with S first and C second, you've got someone for whom diligence and accuracy are supreme. This personality type likes things done in a steady, sequential manner. The SC likes the predictability of a routine and wants you to be there to participate in the routine—an alloy of the task-driven nature of the C personality combined with the people-oriented nature of the S. They like to have all the information before making a decision, and they evaluate their decisions carefully. They are also very sensitive to criticism, as the Steadfast's desire to please combined with the Curator's desire to be accurate make for a delicate balance.

THE CURATOR

It seems apt that the primary traits of the Curator line up neatly in alliteration. The Curator is conscientious, careful, compliant, cautious, circumspect, and concrete. How's that for order and tidiness? The Curator, like the Director, is task-oriented. If you've got a problem that needs to be solved, the Curator is the one to call. He has a strong perfectionist streak, and anything that falls short is very disturbing to him. He really wants to get things right and will work hard toward that goal. One of my daughter's friends has a strong Curator streak. I love it when she comes over because she'll straighten the cabinets and tidy up the pantry.

My daughter Maesyn presents as an almost even blend of Director and Curator. Her Curator traits make her a fantastic student— diligent and meticulous. A couple of my sisters-in-law have strong Curator streaks. They jest that so great is their love of checklists, if they complete tasks that weren't originally on the checklist, they'll go back and add them to the list just so they can cross them off. That's very fulfilling for the Curator.

AGES AND STAGES

You may notice the threads of a Curator very early on. That baby of yours who thrives on a succinct schedule and gets all out of sorts when the schedule gets hijacked? You just might have a Curator in the crib. The toddler who adores a laminated sheet with stickers to assign to a morning and evening routine? Possible Curator territory. A preschooler who loves completing a puzzle but is also capable of a meltdown when a different puzzle proves more difficult to solve? Yep, sounds like a potential Curator. Even at an early age, Curators just have a sense of how an ordered world should be, and anything short of that can make them itch. They may also be the kid who seems to be something of a lone wolf, preferring quieter, more predictable environments over a crowded playground or bustling birthday party.

KNOTS AND NOTS

The Knots of the Curator include her high standards. She brings a high degree of excellence to whatever she's doing. She cares about the small details, about getting it right. One of the Curator's Nots that will require your coaching is her tendency to become upset or grumpy when things aren't going smoothly. She'll need your guidance in remembering to consider others' feelings, as she tends to discount others' emotions in the interest of undertaking the job at hand. It's tough for a Curator to take criticism because getting things right is of such high value to her.

Matthew 25:14–30 is a great parable to help remind your Curator to trust God more than hanging on too tightly to what is known, what is routine, and what seems safe.

THE BLENDS

CD—If your child presented with C first and D second, think of him as a Curating Director. He is doubly task-oriented and driven. This blend finds great fulfillment in the planning and execution of projects. This is the kid who feels he must complete the Lego build from his new set before he does anything else. A child with this blend will often be somewhat reserved, and he has a natural capacity to see problems and improvements that need to be made in any given situation. He'll need encouragement to relax and have fun, as these things don't come easily to him.

CI—If your child shows C as her primary and I as her secondary, she shows strong characteristics of a Curating Inspirer. She has a mix of task-and people-oriented capabilities and can handle big groups as well as enjoy small teams. A child with this blend is somewhat of a ballast in situations—the conscientious, problem-solving manner of the C combines with the influencing nature of the I, allowing her to bring a counterbalance to challenges. In addition, the people skills of the I along with the accuracy of the C allow this blend to read people very well.

CS—In our family of ten—eight kids, two parents—we don't have anyone who comes close to this blend, which is probably a good thing. The general pandemonium of the Carr household would be tough for a true CS to take. This is a personality that likes to do one thing at a time and delights in doing that one thing with great precision. The CS far prefers life to be scheduled and predictable, as a chaotic environment really upsets his apple cart. The CS blend has a strong capacity for serving and for being happy working behind the scenes. Taking risks is not in his wheelhouse.

HOW YOUR OWN PERSONALITY STYLE FACTORS INTO THE MIX

In the previous chapter, I asked you to also take the assessment for yourself. This lets you better understand the curious threads that go into the making of *you*. It's natural for your personality to find it easier to relate to some personalities than to others. And your understanding of your own personality in conjunction with your child's can help both of you sort through conflict and communication.

Let's say you're a strong C—a Curator. And let's say God gave you a child who is a high I—an Inspirer. Your strengths as a Curator are your attention to detail and your desire for things to be done with excellence. When you send your Inspirer to go clean his room, he tears up the stairs, singing loudly and banging doors. He calls down from the top of the stairs several times, excited to tell you the story he thought up while he was trying to clean. And he busts back down the stairs in a handful of minutes, excitedly declaring that he's "done."

You have your doubts.

But you mount the stairs to review his work.

Or lack thereof.

The room looks relatively untouched from its previous looks-like-a-tornado-swept-through status. When you express your irritation with his lack of thoroughness, he looks at you, perplexed. "But, Mom!" he says enthusiastically. "Look! I made a path from the door to the bed and from the bed to the closet. It's all good!"

What's going on here?

Is your Inspirer being obnoxiously disobedient, or is he just being lazy?

While there might be a pinch of either of those thrown in there, that's not all that's going on. For the Inspirer, big picture is where it's at. His God-given bent is to find a creative, interesting solution to problems. His eagerness is for human connection. Spending hours on a mundane chore isn't all that inspiring to him. And you? Your Curator personality allows you to see the way things should be ordered and tell, at a glance, what's not right. Your Inspirer has also been given a gift for peacemaking. He's a natural negotiator, and in carving that path from his door to his bed to his closet, he's created a solution that honors each of you.

Sort of.

So how do you navigate this clash of styles?

Though it may seem impossible, you have some powerful tools at the ready.

Remember, the Inspirer is highly people-oriented. He's not crazy about having to do something on his own. He also likes a stimulating, entertaining environment. If you're willing to make the experience more social and fun, you're much more likely to make progress. The odds that an Inspirer will ever clean a bedroom to your Curator standards are not high. But let's remember what the greater goal is here. You want to help your Inspirer develop a stronger ability to attend to details, to not get sidelined.

So you try again. You go upstairs with your Inspirer. You have him pick out some party music. You ask him to tell you about one toy he can't seem to find. You make it a goal to treasure hunt for that toy. You divide the room into fourths and tell him the goal is to get one-quarter of the room picked up as quickly as possible to see if the toy is there. You honor the bent in him that loves people and fun experiences. You honor the bent in yourself that desires order. And you bend to each other, a mutual respect for the beautiful and diverse personalities God has given each of you.

Or maybe *you're* the people person. You're the Steadfast, the good friend, the diligent worker. And God has placed a Director in your home. You so long to connect with her, but even from toddlerhood, she's never been your snuggler. She's always been on the move, looking for the next obstacle to conquer. And the very force of her personality is completely beyond you. She's willing to dig in, fight, take a stand. You'd much rather everyone just get along. How do you handle your position as the parent to a child whose personality seems so much more forceful than your own?

She's going to grow you as you grow her.

Remember, the Director likes knowing the lay of the land.

She may squawk, she may protest, but at the end of the day, she appreciates clear expectations. A Director in your home can thrive if you're intentional in assigning her a task, asking her to oversee it, and giving her guided authority to complete the task. To try to squash her natural leadership won't develop her strengths, yet to allow that natural leadership to run rampant over your parental authority will facilitate a tyrant. It's a God thing for your child to have Director threads, and it's a God thing for you to help guide that powerful strand.

Directors and Curators are powerfully motivated by tasks and by you entrusting them with projects they can handle confidently.

Inspirers and Steadfasts thrive when motivated by relationship, when people are involved in the process.

Directors and Inspirers respond well when they're allowed to have some lead.

Steadfasts and Curators respond well with consistency and clearly communicated expectations.

If your personality seems to be the opposite of your child's, you're going to have to very intentionally utilize what motivates and inspires him, not what works most comfortably for you. Obviously, there are times when a child is simply being defiant or disobedient. But in my conversations with moms and dads, as they unpack for me their child's behaviors they're concerned about, I usually note several things. First, the parent's expectations about what a child should do or be responsible for are a tad high. And second, these expectations often come from a place of parental preference, not a place of understanding and embracing the unique personality of the child.

I'm not talking about allowing anarchy here. Not at all. When I see kids running amuck and parents vaguely throwing up their hands before returning to regularly scheduled programming, it pains me. But when I see parents calling the strengths in their child's personality things to be conquered or when I see the challenges in a child's bent being called sin, it concerns me that those parents are being blindly reactive to their child's behavior instead of guiding, coaching, and understanding.

A child is not a being to be fixed.

She's a being to be focused.

And there's one more important thing to note.

Just as we've talked through some of the potential tangles we—or our culture—may bring to our parenting, it's possible to use this tool of identifying our child's personality in a way that hems them in and is not helpful. While personality traits may be discernible early in life, we don't want to create a self-fulfilling prophecy. We need to allow our child to continue to show us who he is and to honor who he is becoming.

> **A CHILD IS NOT A BEING TO BE FIXED. SHE'S A BEING TO BE FOCUSED.**

A child's personality is not static. It's a blossoming, growing, developing vivacity, something that should leave room to surprise us and show us new dimensions. To begin to understand someone's temperament is not to affix them to a specimen board and announce, "There! Right there! That's an excellent exhibit giving the full range of this or that temperament." If we go to that place, we've missed the point. We're on a journey to become thread seekers, parents passionate about seeing their kids for who they truly are. Yes, it's helpful to have guidelines that help equip us and our kids to have a fuller understanding of who God created them to be. But just as God has left wiggle room in our genetic signatures for the expression of individuality, so too should we honor that space between what we think we observe in our children and what God has intended to uniquely unfold.

Remember, you're raising an original. And while there will

be familiar framework, the artistry inside is completely ground-breaking. Don't exchange the magnificence of an emerging pearl for something safely predictable.

Also, don't become so consumed with trying to quantify that you miss the beauty of the quest. At the end of the day, what will speak most to your child is not that you could classify her but that you saw her—really saw her—with all of her sharp angles and rounded corners, the friction of her will and the delicacy of her soul.

PART 4

LIVING ORIGINAL

CHAPTER 9

ON OVERLOAD MODE

Evaluating the Extracurricular

While I am busy with little things,
I am not required to do greater things.
Saint Francis de Sales

I WAS absolutely frantic.

Breathlessly dashing from one spot to the next, tossing paperwork, dumping out diaper bags, and emptying pockets, I was also
trying to have an in-depth phone conversation with a friend who
was hurting. I attempted to make the appropriate compassionate
responses, but my mind was in overdrive. Two kids needed to be
driven to dance rehearsal and another to soccer practice—at the
opposite end of town, of course. I'd have just enough time to skid
into a physical therapy session for another child, and in between
I needed to grab a birthday present for a party some of the kids
were attending. Which reminded me I had to pick those kids up
early from a playdate so they could make it to the birthday party.
And then it would be time to pick everyone up from all of the
above—like a motion film run in reverse.

All this was possible . . . if . . .

. . . if I could just find it.

Front door ajar, activity bags and snacks packed, one or two younger kids already in the van screaming from their car seats, clock ticking.

And I couldn't find it anywhere.

Almost in tears, I told my friend I'd be praying for her but right now I needed to be in the car and on my way and I still had to search for my . . . cell phone.

Oh.

I was talking on it.

Which is why it wasn't in my purse, pocket, or diaper bag.

Sometimes overscheduled, activity-laden multitasking can really bite you in the heinie.

AN OVERSCHEDULED GENERATION

Nearly 60 percent of kids in the United States between the ages of six and seventeen are involved in some sort of extracurricular activity. Sports represent the lion's share of that involvement, with lessons and clubs such as music, dance, and Scouts coming in second, according to the latest US census data.[12] Kids who participate in such activities generally perform better academically and also enjoy other benefits, such as improved social engagement and meaningful experiences to include on their college applications.[13] There's convincing research to show that kids thrive with just enough homework and activity to keep them busy—the key phrase being "just enough."

But there's growing concern amongst child development specialists that we're creating an overly stressed, hyper-scheduled, time-starved generation. We've taken something beneficial and expanded it into a bloated buffet of busy. Sleep deprivation, stress, and short tempers abound while sports equipment, permission slips, and costume fees pile up.

Kids are beginning to manifest symptoms of stress typically not encountered until adulthood. Depression, anxiety, and acting out become part of the daily terrain when unrelenting urgency is the pace. And this puts kids at risk for cognitive damage from increased levels of cortisone, the hormone that activates in stressful situations. Blood sugar levels, blood pressure, sleep cycle, and learning retention can all be impacted by a too-crammed agenda with high performance presumptions.

It also turns out that stress is contagious. David Code, author of *Kids Pick Up on Everything: How Parental Stress Is Toxic to Kids*, said in a beliefnet.com interview, "It's ironic: Parents worry about BPA in plastics and chemicals in food, but when it comes to children's health the real toxin is their parents' stress, because kids pick up on everything."[14]

On the crazy days that I can't find my cell phone because I'm talking on it, it's no wonder my kids bicker, cry, and seem far less tolerant and flexible than usual. They've caught my busy bug and are manifesting the symptoms.

Years ago, as I was trying to figure out how to maintain a bit of sanity while administrating our brood, I came across Teri Maxwell's book *Managers of Their Homes*, a how-to guide on scheduling for families. Teri had moms write down every single thing they felt was in their realm of responsibility, from chores to hobbies to sleeping to eating. Moms were then instructed to estimate the daily amount of time each of these things took. And she didn't let you cheat. You had to allow a reasonable amount of time for sleep and self-care. When you finished estimating, you added up all of those times.

The first time I went through the exercise, my estimate was in the mid-thirties. As in *hours*. Per *day*.

Teri said that if you came up with an estimate over twenty-four hours, there were clearly items on that list that were not from God.

Because God makes days twenty-four hours long.

Not thirty-two. Or thirty-three . . . or thirty-four.

Conviction much?

I clearly had way, way more on my plate than even the Day Designer would assign me. I had to do some serious editing to pare things down to a realistic twenty-four-hour period. And that lesson has stayed with me. Now, when stress and bickering and frustration and fatigue dog our days, I know I've once again allowed things to become hyper-scheduled and activity-driven.

Determining what activities our kids should be involved in requires us to take an honest look at some things. First, we need to evaluate our family's season of life. Next, we need to look at the time and resource commitments we're taking on. And then we need to use the information we've gleaned about our kids—what makes them an original, how their personality type responds to certain situations—as another deciding factor. Some kids need lots of unstructured time to rejuvenate. Some need the positive pressure of being lovingly pushed to do something difficult. Some need to learn how to do nothing at all.

Mom and Dad's personalities also come into play. If a tightly packed schedule wears out a parent (such as frantically searching for the very phone you're talking on . . . ahem . . .), that's also a factor. Your child may have broad borders and an amazing ability to deal with all kinds of activity and bustle, but you need to consider yourself as well. It needs to be a complementary dance between parent and child, taxi driver and passenger, financier and recipient.

At the end of the day, there's one critical thing to remember when considering the vast buffet of hobbies, arts, sports, church activities, and all the other good things.

Are you ready?

The thing is not the thing.

Let that soak in for a minute.

The thing is not the thing.

While that may sound like some kind of ancient codex from a *Lord of the Rings* adventure, it's actually pretty simple. Whatever your child is participating in, there needs to be a higher goal. Soccer isn't just about kicking a ball up and down the field—it's about team play and cooperation, physical training, and strategy. Dance isn't just about performing and choreography—it's about strengthening the brain/body connection, discipline, and learning to tell a story through movement and music. The *thing* you're looking for is the character development and growth that comes from well-designed activities guided by caring coaches and instructors.

Also, sometimes you'll need to look outside the traditional activities box. If you want your child to be physically active, it doesn't need to be through the venue of baseball, swimming, or gymnastics. Hiking, running, cycling, tennis, and even geocaching can all develop physical fitness as well as discipline.

Now that we've figured out that *the thing is not the thing*, let's dive in. Instead of adding more, more, more, let's begin by figuring out what is *most*. What is *most* important. What is *most* beneficial. What is *most* powerful in the nurturing of this original being we've been given.

HONESTLY. WHAT'S ON YOUR CALENDAR?

Right now, do a quick assessment. Scan what's on your calendar. Really look at it. I'm not talking about just a vague recall that one of the kids has a practice on Tuesday night and there's some kind of school deal on Wednesday. Look at it in detail. Include the commute time involved. Include the trip to the grocery store to pick up snacks for the track meet. Include how much homework your kids have each night. List it all out on paper.

Even though I keep a robust calendar, I can have selective amnesia about the outlying time commitments inherited when we add another activity to the mix. Extra permission slips to fill out. A drive across town to pick up the costume piece. That last-minute rehearsal. The game that got rained out two weeks ago and is now being rescheduled for the week we're supposed to be out of town.

And honestly, what is the academic situation like for your kids? I know many, many parents who have placed their children in academically rigorous schools, with educational experiences that require lots of homework and memorization and science fair projects that look like marketing proposals for major tech companies. They've signed those same kids up for activities and practices that last late into the evening—every night of the week. And they become frustrated and worried when their kids' grades start to suffer.

Can I lovingly inject a little sanity and common sense into your life? If you're going to put your child in a school environment with that level of homework, you're going to have to cut back on the activities.

With our daughter McKenna's dance experience, there came a point where it simply wasn't sustainable for several of her classmates. Our homeschool schedule afforded us better flexibility to continue with the rigorous schedule, but many of her friends who ultimately ended up quitting dance would go to the studio straight from school and stay there until 9:00 or 10:00 at night, three or four nights a week. The pressures of their junior and senior years of high school began to catch up with the heavy dance commitment.

Parents sometimes think they're managing their time well if they limit each child to just one extracurricular activity. But be aware—there's a wide range of commitment when it comes to sports, arts, and hobbies. McKenna "only" participated in competitive dance, but that one "activity" involved nightly classes and rehearsals, weekend trips traveling across the region to conventions and competitions, and summers spent at dance intensives and training at Joffrey Ballet in New York City. Also, the price tag for this one activity was a serious line-item on our family budget. A once-a-week, thirty-minute guitar lesson is a far different animal than playing on a select sports team or having the lead in a musical that runs for a month.

Remember, it's simple math. There are twenty-four hours in a day. Not thirty-two . . . or thirty-three . . . or thirty-four.

HONESTLY. WHAT IS YOUR SEASON RIGHT NOW?

I've had the conversation more than once. An exhausted mom approaches me after I've spoken at an event. She's sporting fatigue shiners under red-veined eyes and carries a to-go coffee cup that holds about a liter of caffeine. She tells me she can't imagine running a crew my size, that she's completely wiped out with just one or two kids. I, in turn, ask her to tell me about her days. And she begins the litany. Gymnastics practice. Swimming lessons. Playgroup. Library day. Tutoring. Music class.

And then I ask her one simple question: "How old is your child?"

She responds that her child is three years old. Or two. Or even a year or six months.

She's doing this to herself. Because, news flash—that pre-K

kid is most likely not even going to remember all this running around, Mommy-and-Me class craziness.

It's easier to see it when kids are younger and to find the humor in someone making the toddler years crazy before the realities of school and club soccer and college prep hit. But in the process of evaluating what bandwidth our families have for more classes, more practices, more hobbies, what is it that we want most in this season with our kids?

If you're working away from home the majority of the day and your younger kids are spending most of their day in child-care, don't compromise critical family time together by adding in baby ballet and toddler gym classes. Spending time with *you* is what's most important at these ages, not running off to one more place so they can hang out with other toddlers. If your kids are in traditional all-day school settings, hanging out with you is critical—and not just chatting in the car while heading to the next activity. If your family is going through a season of transition or challenge, establishing margin to your days is essential. If you've just added a new baby to the mix, skipping one season of soccer isn't going to forever impair your child's game.

HONESTLY. WHAT ARE YOU TEACHING YOUR KIDS ABOUT TIME?

This verse.

It gets me.

"Teach us to number our days, that we may gain a heart of wisdom" (Psalm 90:12).

I also love the way *The Message* says it: "Oh! Teach us to live well! Teach us to live wisely and well!"

My kids are watching me. Learning from me. Figuring out

how to spend this incredible, fleeting thing called time. They're noticing the pace of our home and seeing what activities Michael and I have deemed important enough to make the calendar.

I want to make sure they're noticing that the way we spend our seconds is infused with wisdom. Yes, I know that sometimes I've shown them how to infuse a day with an absurd amount of busyness. But God often speaks of living out the span of our days with wisdom. Jesus's brother James gives us a good baseline for our planning and scheduling and calendaring when he says, "Now listen, you who say, 'Today or tomorrow we will go to this or that city, spend a year there, carry on business and make money.' Why, you do not even know what will happen tomorrow. What is your life? You are a mist that appears for a little while and then vanishes. Instead, you ought to say, 'If it is the Lord's will, we will live and do this or that'" (James 4:13–15).

Our days belong to God—to His intent and to His will. As much as we want to encourage our kids to find their own unique avenues, to flourish as one of God's originals means entrusting the days, the hours, the minutes, the seconds, into His leading.

And there's something else.

God has this thing about rest.

As in, He rested.

And He commands us to rest too.

It's one of the Big Ten—those commandments that shaped the nation of Israel. It's intended as an incredible blessing—a gift of refreshing and reframing. Our kids need to see some sort of Sabbath modeled. They need to place it in the fervor of their schedules. They need to see us practice it. And while I don't promote a particular model of what it should look like for your family, it does need to be there.

Sundays are busy around here. Since I'm in ministry, the day begins early, and it demands a considerable amount of attention.

But almost every week, Sunday is also the day we come home, eat some lunch, and head for naps. Sunday naps. Love 'em. They're a gift. And they do speak the sanction of Sabbath. We don't always get it right, of course. Some Sundays there's a performance or a baby shower on the calendar. But the Sunday nap is now firmly infused into our family's culture—a culture that tends to be far more frenetic than placid.

Because we're raising originals in a time when there's more entertainment, more distractions, and more access to activities than ever, we'll need to show our originals the beauty of boredom and the possibilities of unstructured time. Some of our most creative moments, some of our biggest adventures and most boisterous laughs, have arrived courtesy of a clear day on the calendar—a day when we could have pacified the boredom with another movie, another errand, another chore. Instead, we got comfortable with the comma, the pause in the paragraph of our life narrative.

Not every space on the calendar needs to be filled in. Not every afternoon needs to include a carpool. Not every Saturday needs a tournament.

SO HOW DO I MAKE CHOICES?

Whatever we're going to spend our time and resources on when it comes to kid activities, we need to make sure it counts. After all, time is precious and finances must be managed. While it's fine to try a potpourri of possibilities to determine where a kid's interests and natural talents may lie, at some point it must mean more than one more place to be and one more check to write.

Before you start making some choices, do one thing first: Ask your child. See what she has to say. And as you're listening to her answer, remember, *the thing is not the thing.* If the goal is helping your child develop a lifelong habit of physical fitness, that can be accomplished in a number of ways. It doesn't have to be soccer. Or T-ball. Or basketball. It can be a hiking club or an acrobatic trampoline class or lap swimming with you. Allow him to choose from a number of options, any of which can accomplish *the thing*.

After you and your child have talked, research what you're getting into. Make sure you understand the costs, time requirements, and tournament or competition schedule. In the early years with my younger kids, I'd make a phone call to, say, a gymnastics program and find out the monthly tuition. Great. Looked like it would fit into the budget, as long as we skipped the cable subscription. We'd attend the first few classes before discovering we also needed to purchase a particular leotard or jacket or equipment bag needed for—gasp!—an upcoming competition requiring an overnight stay in a hotel.

Hmmm . . .

Maybe we should have subscribed to cable and watched gymnastics on a sports channel instead.

I've seen families pour incredible amounts of time and money into a sport or hobby for their child, all at the peril of future fiscal responsibility. Sometimes they believed their child possessed a truly unique ability that required this kind of training and outlay. Sports in particular seems to be the primary area where parents hold tight to the dream that their kid could go pro. Maybe for a few kids that's true, but the odds are truly infinitesimal for a career in pro sports. If that's the only goal out there as your child runs the frenzied race of school and then homework and then practice, it might be time to rethink things. Yes, let's help our kids dream big, but a dream that becomes an idol can eat the heart out of the bearer.

What about those activities you'd like your kid to participate in, but he doesn't want to play along? I know, I know—some parents out there believe it's important to force-feed their kid an activity they've deemed critical and important and essential, be it playing the piano or playing on a sports team. But after all the work we've done to understand our children better and all we've learned about the importance of seeing who they truly are, a heavy-handed push toward the extracurricular can be a great recipe for frustration, rebellion, and tears. I've seen parents insist on piano lessons, only to end up with a kid who hates music. I've seen kids forced onto a soccer field who end up resisting sports in general.

We've got to give some honor to the threads of originality in each of our children. The Director needs to feel like she has a voice in choosing her activities. The Inspirer will thrive best in people-centered events, not solitary lessons that require lots of lonely practice. The Steadfast can find great fulfillment in a team environment that is supportive and consistent but will be deeply hurt in a stressful, critical setting. The Curator can blossom well in an activity or sport where the objective is clear and the opportunity to find solutions presents itself.

Let's be willing to think outside the box when it comes to activities as well. Our culture has elevated sports to the point where it often seems to be the only game out there (pun intended). But I've had the delight of seeing Steadfasts or Curators excel in Kinect workshops and camps, building incredible structures with creativity and innovation. Chess clubs, American Sign Language classes, and photography lessons are just a few possibilities that could be a good fit for your original. Piano is not the only instrument upon which people learn music. Engage in some research to find activities that may be off the beaten path but could be the perfect fit for your family goals.

Sometimes a certain activity can seem like a great way for our kids to develop strength in an area that's a challenge for their personality style. And it can be. But that expectation should be clearly defined and communicated with a coach or instructor ahead of time. My youngest daughter, Merci, tends not to like being pushed physically. I think it comes down to a couple of factors—she doesn't like to be wrong or critiqued, and the stroke she experienced at birth makes her learning curve for certain activities pretty steep. We put her in gymnastics for a while, but I took time to thoroughly interview her potential instructors. We talked about where they should really push her but also what would cause her to shut down.

Which brings up another important point. When you add in that extracurricular, you're adding more people to your world, to your community. You're allowing more people access to your calendar and your priorities. And sometimes that may take some editing as well.

SOMETIMES, YOU GOTTA FIRE THE COACH

When I was a freshman in high school, I decided to try out for volleyball. I hadn't played before, but several of my friends loved the sport and the uniforms were pretty cute, so I thought it might be a good fit for me. I made the frosh team along with several of my buddies and began to learn the lingo and rules of the sport. Since we were the entry-level team, with the JV and varsity players boasting far superior skills, it seemed reasonable that there wouldn't be much pressure on us. After all, we were just beginning our volleyball careers.

However, nobody shared that fact with our ambitious coach. Who seemed to also have some anger issues, in addition to being crazy-driven. She was a tiny little thing with an enviable tan, a carefully tended spiral perm, and a personality that was a barely contained cauldron of rage, a lava flow of lividness sloshing onto the volleyball court.

Practices were an exercise in screaming and yelling and general hostility. During games—with parents watching—she controlled herself a little better, but not by much. In the locker room after a match, she'd rant and rave and call out specific players she felt were "idiots" or "stupid."

During an away game, we played our hearts out against a highly competitive team. We had some good moments, but in the end we pretty much had our hats handed to us. As we boarded the team bus to head home, our coach railed and screamed and pitched a fit. We sat, heads hung, sweaty and tired, just ready to eat some dinner and listen to Foreigner on our Walkmans—that ancient technology for personal music listening that utilized cassette tapes and reams of batteries.

But our coach wasn't done with us yet.

Because of our poor performance, she declared, we wouldn't be stopping for dinner. We hadn't earned that right. Maybe, she hoped, we'd take this punishment to heart and step up our game the next time around.

We arrived back at our high school to parents waiting in cars to ferry us home. My mom, noting the general countenance of the team, asked me what was up when I got in the car. I gave her a brief thumbnail of the day but was too tired and was feeling too weird to fill in much detail. With my head lolling against the headrest of the passenger seat, I mentioned that the team had been denied dinner. My mom immediately peeled into a drive-thru to grab some food, mothering instincts on high alert.

As a high school freshman who enjoyed a ridiculously fast metabolism and thought my skinny legs and frame a curse (oh, how I long for those days now), I could go into a low blood sugar spiral very quickly. My speech slowed and my fuzzy head felt more and more convoluted, and even the tempting scent of hot French fries tickling my nostrils didn't help. By the time we arrived home, I was sick as a dog, unable to keep anything down, and was forced to sip drops of apple juice throughout the long night to try to get my blood sugar back up.

To say my mother was livid wouldn't quite capture the vivid hues and textures of her response.

My parents raised us with the ethic that you don't quit just because things get tough. And generally, they held us to that. But as they navigated the whitecap waters of coaches and club leaders and teachers who varied wildly in their skill sets and personalities, there were times when quitting actually represented the higher ethic. It didn't happen often and it didn't dilute the overall message of hanging in even when things got tough. Over the years, though, a few situations presented themselves that required a sea change.

One was my brother's militant Boy Scout leader who literally wore Scout emblem-emblazoned boxer shorts. I kid you not.

The other was my frosh volleyball coach.

Prior to the enforced losers' fast, I'd told my folks about the coach's behavior. They'd encouraged me to take her criticism and use it to get better, to bring a more aggressive approach to my game. But the day after the hungry bus ride home and my low blood sugar-induced illness, I begged my parents to let me quit the team. The level of stress and demoralization had made the experience miserable.

My parents agreed, with this caveat: I would need to be the one to tell my coach. It was a piece of genius, really. I was at an age where this would be a valuable lesson in walking away from a situation that wasn't working and in learning to do that with respect, candor, and grace. It also gave my parents a gauge as to how sincere I was about quitting, as it would be no small task to confront this wrathful volleyball combatant.

I went through the rigors of one more practice and then asked to speak privately with my coach. I told her I would be quitting the team, that it just didn't seem I was cut out for volleyball, especially her style of it—the intensity, the pressure. She seemed genuinely surprised and told me she thought I had great promise as a player. Her trademark anger seemed to simmer just below the surface as she made some catty comments about quitters and losers, and she pressured me to reconsider. I remained resolute. I left her office feeling lighter, happier, and more mature.

Sometimes, it takes more courage to quit than to continue.

While I do think it's important to teach kids the value of staying the course, if we have clear family priorities and understand the real takeaway from each extracurricular activity, we'll know what to do when a situation gets sticky.

> SOMETIMES, IT TAKES MORE COURAGE TO QUIT THAN TO CONTINUE.

We sometimes treat coaches or instructors as if they're the Lord's anointed, as if they hold the key to our child's future, but actually God is the one who holds the key. And He can work far beyond the ability and web of a well-connected instructor.

And then there's this.

You don't need permission from your kid's coach to live your values.

Let me show you what I mean.

One amazing day, some of our best friends were bringing their new son—an amazing bundle of frenetic joy named Jonathan—home from Ethiopia. We'd been heavily involved in Jonathan's adoption process and were beyond excited that this little guy was finally on his way home to his family. His adoption was a beautiful and complex endeavor into which our beloved friends had poured time and resources and heart and faith. And because our friends live just a few doors down from us and we run in and out of each other's homes with full family rights, by extension this little guy was arriving into our family as well. Once we got the arrival date and time of the flight in from Africa, we cleared our schedule so we could head to the airport with celebratory signs and balloons. One of my kids made sure to mention to an instructor that she would be missing that day's rehearsal because of Jonathan's homecoming.

The instructor was not happy. At all. She questioned why my kid couldn't just wait until the next day to meet Jonathan. She couldn't understand why someone would skip a rehearsal for such an event as an adoption homecoming. She suggested that my kid's priorities weren't in line with what it "takes" to perform at the highest level.

Well, now.

As a family—when it comes to activities and hobbies—we're very clear.

People matter more than projects, performances, and perfect attendance.

There it is. Simple.

Now, don't get me wrong. When you've assured people you'll show up, when you've committed to a performance, when you've given your word, it's not okay to be flaky and leave people hanging. Because people *are* the value. And when someone is fickle with their commitment and leaves the team short, people are being devalued.

But because people are the value, when an important event arrives for the people you love—when there's an opportunity to celebrate life and experience community and show others how much you treasure them—missing an extra practice or rehearsal can't even compete. And it shouldn't.

We've seen coaches and instructors throw fits and threaten positions and hold grudges because families attended weddings or took vacations or visited grandparents.

Um . . . not okay.

That kind of coach or instructor is teaching kids that performance is more important than people. And as per our family culture, that's not going to fly.

On occasion, you may have to fire that person from your kid's life.

Making these kinds of changes shouldn't be frequent. If you find you can't seem to get along with most of your children's instructors, it might be time to dig that compact mirror out of your purse and take a good, hard look.

It might just be you.

But if overall the people guiding your kids through sports and hobbies and the arts are an enjoyable part of your extended community, you'll feel confident in walking away when a tyrant shows up. And learn to look for signs of a tyrant. Whenever possible, get clear on who you're initially hiring—even volunteers—to work with your kid. As a friend of mine says, if you choose a porcupine, you can't be mad when it acts like a porcupine. If you choose a coach who has a reputation for turning out a winning team but is also known for being verbally hostile and having overly long practices, you can't be irritated when that becomes your kid's experience. If you choose a dance school that displays all kinds of shiny trophies but doesn't know the meaning of an excused absence and motivates through belligerence, don't be shocked when that becomes your kid's experience. A porcupine is a porcupine, not a kitten.

There's something else.

If you choose an instructor and environment for your child that's reputed to be nurturing and laid-back, comfortable and easygoing, you don't get to be huffy about a less-than-stellar victory record or a more lackadaisical approach to organization. Familial freedom may mean fewer shiny trophies on the shelf but greater treasures in the memory bank.

THE COURAGE TO HAVE THE CONVERSATION

That collision of our own interests and dreams and those of our kids? Sometimes we'd rather just not know.

Our friend Adam was a talented baseball player back in the day. He enjoyed a gilded high school career and adores, adores, adores the game. The fresh green of the field. The crisp white chalk lines marking paths to the bases. The crack of the bat. The hot dogs. The music. It's been a lifelong love affair.

His son Colby has been graced with a long, lanky build and a precision arm. A natural athlete, Colby's been playing the game since he could toddle up to the T-ball tee. He played several seasons of select baseball—with all its back-to-back practices, travel, and tournaments. Adam loved seeing his son play at that level, and Colby was doing well on the field.

Then Adam had the courage to have the conversation.

The conversation in which he actually sat down and asked Colby about his baseball goals.

And then Adam had the courage to listen.

To intentionally, fully engage in listening to Colby's answer.

As it turned out, Colby really enjoys playing baseball. But he doesn't dream of taking his game to a higher level. He's just as happy on the rec team as he is on the select team. And he likes to play basketball as well. And swim. And have time to hang out with friends and go fishing with his dad and brother.

So, in terms of wanting a select baseball career, that would be a no.

Baseball in general? Sure.

I was so impacted by Adam's willingness to have that conversation with his son, especially knowing how much the game has meant to Adam. Colby hadn't been resisting the select team experience. He hadn't been acting out or asking to scale things back. But Adam still opened the door for the conversation to happen and then was willing to adjust to a baseball experience that matched Colby's aspirations.

That kind of conversation requires courage for any of us who have hoped to see our kids go far in a particular sport or endeavor.

KNOWING WHEN TO PUSH

Each child God has placed in our lives—whether we are parents, grandparents, teachers, mentors, or extended family—has been given a unique gift and contribution to be realized in this world. Sometimes that gifting, that contribution, is one that takes a tremendous amount of coaching and mentoring. Sometimes that coaching and mentoring takes a great deal of time. And discipline. And focus. Sometimes there is great joy in the doing. Sometimes it's downright hard. Sometimes it competes with other great endeavors and opportunities.

All that said, how do we guide our kids to remain, to abide?

We faced this situation with our second daughter, McKenna. As she entered her preteen years, I was somewhat startled to realize she was becoming a gifted dancer. I myself wasn't raised dancing, had never had a dance lesson. So I didn't really know what I was looking at when I watched my kids dance. I knew I loved seeing them perform, but I didn't have any knowledge about what I was observing.

Although McKenna's talent for dance came as a surprise at the time, in retrospect it makes much more sense. She's always been a disciplined, intentional, keenly observant and kinesthetic individual—the very building blocks of an athlete. What I hadn't recognized in her was the deep passion for dance that had begun to emerge. We'd been doing dance for "fun," for performance experience, and because her older sister enjoyed the activity and she'd come along for the ride.

But now, as McKenna continued to mature in her sport, we started to realize we were seeing something that could be part of her purpose, her contribution in this season.

We asked for input from dance teachers, choreographers, master instructors. They all saw something in McKenna as well. We upped the amount of time at the studio, let her spend summers at dance intensives, communicated our belief to her that we thought she could go far with dance, that she seemed to be one of those people who might just have found her "thing" at an early age. She was finishing her sophomore year of high school, with a few more years of training ahead of her before launching into the professional arena, when something happened.

A devastating earthquake in Haiti.

McKenna was transfixed. She was deeply impacted by what she was seeing on news reports, from accounts being brought back to us from one of the nonprofits our church supports in Port au Prince. A mission trip began to be organized, and McKenna gathered all the information she could about what it would take to go and the kind of funds needed to be raised.

At some point, we pulled out our calendars and started looking at dates for the trip.

The Haiti mission trip was going to fall squarely right smack in the center of McKenna's convention and competition season.

McKenna wrestled with what to do. Drawn to the situation in Haiti, it seemed the much more noble thing to skip out on her junior year of the dance performance team. Was it selfish to stay focused on dance? What kind of help could she provide if she went to Haiti? As we talked and reflected and prayed, McKenna mentioned that her purpose in going on the trip would be to minister to people.

That word.

Minister.

It changed the context of the conversation.

McKenna had been interacting consistently with members of her performance company. Several of the young people on the team were struggling with a variety of problems. Eating disorders. Identity issues. Drug and alcohol abuse. Sexual experimentation. Deep questions about faith and God. McKenna was a calm in the storm for many members of her team, the person to whom they would come with challenges, heartaches, and questions.

That word *minister* made us reconsider her plan to put down dance and travel to Haiti. Michael and I strongly encouraged her to evaluate the ministry she was already engaged in with her dance peers. We pushed her to stay in training, to remain in the group where she'd been placed. We told her she could help support those headed to Haiti while continuing to connect with the people she was currently ministering to. And God directly answered, in the way that He sometimes does.

McKenna raised money for Haiti. She helped fund several relief trips for various groups.

And she stayed in the dance game.

And ministered.

Years later, we can look back and see the power of that moment, that parental push. Several of the people McKenna danced with came to faith in those years that she completed her training. She continues to disciple and love her fellow creatives. Through her time at the Joffrey Ballet intensive in New York City, and through other dance venues, McKenna was able to— and continues to—minister. That advocacy piece, that part of her that responds strongly to wanting to help others, had found an outlet in a unique way. She currently directs a nonprofit, called 2dance2dream, which provides dance instruction for individuals with special needs. (You can read more at 2dance2dream.org.)

In 2014 God opened the door for her to go to Uganda on a mission trip, where she was able to give dance instruction to scores of young people and share the gospel with them. And in 2015, McKenna traveled to Thailand and taught dance to individuals with special needs.

There is sometimes a time to push, to encourage our kids to stay the course, to keep training, to keep going, to keep the focus.

HAVING FUN IS IMPORTANT TOO

Is anybody having fun anymore?

It's a somewhat repetitive platitude. But oft-repeated platitudes usually speak some truth.

The years our children are children are a blink of the eye.

Childhood is a brilliant, dizzying sprint.

As Gretchen Rubin writes, "The days are long, but the years are short."

And while I'm sharing favorite quotes, here's one from Evelyn Nown: "Perhaps parents would enjoy their children more if they stopped to realize the film of childhood can never be run through for a second showing."

My pregnancies always seemed long, particularly the ones that culminated with delivery dates in the hot Oklahoma and Texas summers. But that first year of each of my kids' lives? We were blowing out candles on birthday cakes before I could even process it.

Packed planners and highly scheduled days make that calendar flip even more quickly.

So if we're going to spend irreplaceable time on activities and classes and practices, shouldn't they at least be fun? I know the interest in something has just about run its course when we're getting ready to head out the door and there are complaints, tears, and fatigue. Our sixth child, Journey, has a pretty remarkable gift in a particular area, but we hit a point a few years ago when she just wasn't having fun anymore. Tears accompanied leaving for rehearsals. Stress swirled before competitions. What had been a joy had become a drag. It was hard, but she took a couple years off. Now she's back in, loving her training and its impact on her gifting more than ever. We let the field go fallow for a bit so the nurturing aspects could replenish.

EVALUATING EXTRACURRICULAR ACTIVITIES

I'm a believer in putting pen to paper, in mapping out a decision tree when it comes to getting clear on calendars and sports and camps and competitions and the rest.

Our family has gotten pretty good at weighing what makes the cut and what doesn't. And we do it by asking questions—lots of questions:

- What is *the thing* I want my child to get out of this experience? What benefits do I believe this activity has? What are other activities that could have the same kind of benefits?
- Is this something my child wants to do, or is it something I want him to do?
- Is there something my child wants to do that I don't want her to do? What is it? (Things to ask yourself: Am I hesitant? Can I honestly say my hesitancy does not lie in the tangles of vocation, education, self, or bubble wrap? See chapters 3-6.)

- What is the commitment level required for this activity? How many days a week? What is the drive time? What is the financial responsibility?
- What are we willing to give up in order to facilitate this activity?
- In the activities we currently have in place, is *the thing* happening? Can I see the benefits playing out in my child's life? Or do I seem to be the one more attached to the activity itself and my social connections with other parents?
- When will my child have time for free play? for social life? for church involvement? for quiet time? And when will I?

When determining what to put on your family's calendar, you don't necessarily need to pare down your child's schedule or limit activities, although that might need to happen. What you do need to do is search deeper. If your child is an amazing athlete and your afternoons and weekends and free time and finances are all going toward the nurturing of that talent, what happens if your child blows a knee during a scrimmage? What if, in that one moment of a torn tendon, the scholarship plans and pro career go up in a haze of doctor bills? Does your child know that what's most valuable in his gift is the discipline, the drive, the heart he has carried into every game? Have you equipped your child for a vision of what might come after this activity, this sport, this hobby she dearly loves? Have you helped him know that while this activity is a celebrated part of his life, it doesn't define him?

Remember that painting I told you about in chapter 1, Vermeer's *La Dentellière*? Part of what is considered the genius of the composition is its simple, unadorned background. Because Vermeer kept the background "noise" to a minimum in the painting, you can really focus on what is most important—the beautiful figure of the lacemaker and the lace she is so carefully creating. It challenges me to ask myself what I can eliminate from the "background" of my life to allow me to focus on what is most important. And to take a look at my calendar to see what clutter may be taking up too much of the canvas of my family life.

It seems fitting to close out this chapter with a cry from the heart: *God, please teach us to count, to plan, to lay out our days with wisdom. You've made us the ones who decide what fills up the treasured days of our kids' childhoods. Help us to choose wisely. Amen.*

CHAPTER 10

PURPOSED, NOT PERFECT

Our strength grows out of our weaknesses.
Ralph Waldo Emerson

IT HAD BEEN a hard day.

Really hard.

I was sitting in a soundproof booth, a thick panel of glass in front of me, a silent window to the room outside this chamber. Over my right shoulder was a large speaker with a creepy-looking mechanical toy monkey sitting on top of it, ready to clash the cymbals clasped in his hands. Over my left shoulder was another large speaker, and on top of it sat a small mechanical dog holding drumsticks, poised to strike the small drum in front of him.

On my lap sat my fourth child, two-and-a-half-year-old daughter Maesyn. She leaned back comfortably on the pregnant mound of my stomach, calm and happy, a sharp contrast to my wildly beating heart.

Inside, I was unraveling.

Stunningly, shockingly unraveling.

A few months ago, I'd taken Maesyn to our pediatrician for a routine checkup. At the appointment, I mentioned that I was concerned Maesyn didn't seem to be developing language as quickly as my other kids had. The doctor looked Maesyn over and chuckled, implying that my expectations were a little high, given that some of my other kids had talked really, really early and were probably doing all the talking for Maesyn now. She proclaimed Maesyn perfectly healthy—good eyes, good ears, good reflexes—and sent us on our way.

Six months later, I was still having some concerns. Back to the pediatrician we went, who was still unconcerned but recommended I make an appointment with a developmental specialist in town, just for this nervous mommy's peace of mind. Giving Maesyn another quick vision test, she told me to drop by the audiologist's office to check a hearing test off the list before heading to the developmental specialist. Most likely, she reassured me, Maesyn just needed a little speech therapy to kick-start her vocabulary. No biggie.

Except now the nervous mommy was sitting in an audio booth watching her child not respond to many of the tones and sounds coming from the big speakers with their eerie monkey and toy dog. Frantically staring at the audiologist on the other side of the thick window, I tried to discern any clue from his flat expression. This was supposed to be a simple step on the path to speech therapy, not an experience in failing a hearing test.

Not a revelation.

Not a game changer.

But it was.

At some point, the test ended and the audiologist pulled open the heavy, soundproof door, a soft whoosh of air swirling into the booth. I stood, shifting Maesyn to my hip, panic and claustrophobia setting in. As I stepped down from the booth, the audiologist pushed his glasses back up on the bridge of his nose, blinked dryly, and said, "Well, obviously she's deaf. We'll put her on antibiotics for a couple weeks to make sure it's not an ear infection . . . which it's not. Then you'll come back and we'll see what's next."

Bless him. But not the best booth-side manner.

I put Maesyn down, gathered my purse and Maesyn's little bag of toys, and wandered down the hall to the appointment desk. Gathering the prescription slip and the appointment reminder card, I took Maesyn's hand and reeled into the parking lot, mind simultaneously cacophonous and silent, fragments of questions welling and staunching. I got my little girl strapped into her car seat, her smile wide and gorgeous gray-blue eyes merry under her pigtails. Then I picked up my cellphone to call Michael, unsure how to phrase this kind of news. How did you let your spouse know his child couldn't hear? I'd never seen that one covered in the marriage books.

And, inexplicably, the biggest question rolling around in my head was, *Does this mean Maesyn will have to wear hearing aids to prom?*

Prom?

I was worried about prom?

An event that wouldn't potentially be penciled in on the calendar for another fifteen years. I was worried about a school dance? What kind of crazy person was I? Not to mention we homeschooled, which meant a decided lack of traditional high school prom.

We drove for a bit, tears pooling under the rims of my sunglasses. Maesyn giggled and looked out the window and jabbered away. I wondered about prom a little longer as I glimpsed my gorgeous girl in the rearview mirror.

I found a sliver of resolve.

And I picked up the phone to call Michael.

A new chapter had just begun.

All eight of my babies were pronounced normal, healthy children at birth. And from a medical standpoint, for six of them, that held true. But then Maesyn was diagnosed with significant hearing loss. And at the age of twelve months, our seventh child, Merci, was found to have experienced an ischemic neonatal stroke, resulting in extreme weakness on her left side, commonly referred to as cerebral palsy or hemiplegia.

With each girl, we began the process of searching for terrific therapists, appropriate equipment, and reams of information. We threw ourselves into giving each girl the strongest opportunity to lead "normal" lives in spite of their "not normal" situations. We would ultimately learn the naiveté of that philosophy—and that there are no shortcuts. With Maesyn, it was a steep onramp with major decisions to make. Would we go with a sign language–based communication system, or would we push for spoken language? We discovered that most medical insurance companies don't pay for hearing aids. We had a plethora of educational, financial, speech, and technology choices to make—all of them critical, all of them being made by complete novices to this world.

When we discovered Merci's challenges, we were more sea-soned, more acclimated to the swift process of educating ourselves and quickly making decisions. Our entire family dove into the world of physical and occupational therapy, several of the kids joining Merci and me at appointments so they could learn how to work with her at home on her exercises. We tried some new approaches, like the onabotulinumtoxinA (Botox) procedures I mentioned earlier. We made incremental progress—slow, some-what steady, always challenging.

Both situations required lots of diligence, lots of patience, lots of prayer. To watch your daughters at such young ages struggle and work so much harder than other kids was just plain hard. There were times, in the midst of a tough therapy session, I'd keep my game face intact, only to head straight for my room when we got home, tears falling, words inadequate, heart aching. The days that their struggles overlapped—when Merci's left-side muscles twisted her arm and leg in painful cramps and when Maesyn felt the full frustration of fractured parlance—well, those days were a double whammy.

That's the backstory to this next particular hard day—a day that had been many days in the making.

IN MY PRAYER CLOSET

My prayer closet is often a bathtub filled with bubbles. And it was while soaking in this prayer closet, at the end of this next particular hard day, that I found the words of Psalm 139:13 echoing in my head, a cadence that seemed almost taunting.

"You knit me together . . . . You knit me together. . . . You knit me together . . . ."

So what happened, Lord? I demanded. *What happened when You were knitting Maesyn and Merci together? Did You just drop a stitch?*

And almost immediately, I heard the timbre of God's voice echo in my aching heart, the impression of thought that appears with comprehensive clarity.

Yes. Yes, I did drop a stitch. And would you like to know why?

It just got real.

Yes, sir, I replied.

It's a simple thing to knit row upon row. But when you want to create something of greater purpose, of greater function, you drop stitches. You can then make a cuff, a sleeve, a banding for buttonholes—something that has a more specific use. So yes, I did drop stitches because I have specific intent.

Oh.

I mulled that over, soaking in bubbles and epiphany, soap and insight, lavender and vision, in my tub-shaped prayer closet. I felt profoundly convicted, slightly abashed, and delicately prompted. God had not, in a moment of distraction, let His eye wander from His work.

He had counted the stitches, considered the cost, woven purpose into what some would see as accident. What some would see as weakness. What some would see as damage. But if I was willing to look with a right heart, I would find Him there.

He wasn't done with me yet.

As the waters of my prayer closet washed over my stress and fear, God showed me something more, something that had been in front of me all along but I'd failed to see. He baptized me into a new way of seeing what He was up to, immersing me and raising me to a whispered understanding of the way in which He sometimes chooses to work.

All of us, all of our children, have special needs.

We all have areas—in character, in physicality, in personality, in soul, in cognition, in our individual histories—in which we struggle, we stumble, we stutter.

We all have areas where we think the Lord may have dropped a stitch while He was knitting us.

And He did.

For this purpose: ". . . he said to me, 'My grace is sufficient for you, for my power is made perfect in weakness.' Therefore I will boast all the more gladly about my weaknesses, so that Christ's power may rest on me. That is why, for Christ's sake, I delight in weaknesses, in insults, in hardships, in persecutions, in difficulties. For when I am weak, then I am strong" (2 Corinthians 12:9–10).

When it comes to knitting, dropping stitches has been God's style all along.

It's not enough to know where threads of strength and gifting are. We need to know where the dropped stitches, the frayed fibers, and the thin places are in order to truly understand the fuller canvas of purpose—both our own and our children's.

ALL KIDS HAVE SPECIAL NEEDS

We see ten fingers and ten toes in the delivery room, and we glow at high Apgar results. We proclaim it a blessing. It is. But it is no less a blessing to be entrusted with a child who was knit with physical or cognitive or personality style challenges. We've learned in our journey that all kids have special needs.

Those needs may not be physical or cognitive, but every child comes to this earth with a special need to have their strengths discovered and shaped and their challenges recognized and coached. As the treasures our children are, every precious gemstone is faceted differently to capture the light. If we insist on trying only to maintain a standard of "normal" in our children, we miss the amazing opportunity to coax true brilliance—the brightness of a completely unique soul—to its full purpose.

It's the warning label, the disclaimer I want to place on the previous chapters that have helped us develop a fuller understanding of our kids. It would be easy to grab at the threads of their strengths—those Directors with their ability to conquer big tasks, those Inspirers who can ignite a movement, those Steadfasts who quietly make things happen behind the scenes, those Curators who know how to dig in and accomplish things. It would be easy to select those strands that seem to have success stamped into their fibers and start to weave plans for education and activities and future.

But it would make for a one-dimensional approach.

Have you ever noticed? God is all about paradoxes. He puts them everywhere in creation. Light is both a wave and a particle.

Water can be a vapor, a solid, a liquid. Things that shouldn't be able to exist at the same time do. The deeper we're able to go in our mathematical and theoretical peeping into the universe, the more we keep finding those phenomena that resist our linear suppositions.

God does it with people too. He sends Jesus as a king. A king without a country. A king without a crown. A king without a monarchal line. A king with no army.

A king He is.

A Prince of Peace who brings a sword.

God's Word is filled with people who possess the natural skill sets and abilities to elevate them to key positions—and God skips over those gifted individuals in favor of the wallflower, the stutterer, the 'fraidy cat. God's placement strategy often doesn't match up well with job assessments, strength inventories, and the predictable. Sometimes, in just the place where it seems God has dropped a stitch, He's up to something of tremendous purpose.

Yes, your child's strengths within her temperament and her talents may be the things you find easiest to be proud of. But what you might see as her weaknesses may hold incredible potential. Her weaknesses may hold treasure. Her weaknesses may just hold inklings of her direction.

Which would make those weaknesses powerful strengths.

Especially when her life is being woven by an intentional God.

Because He's definitely got a track record of doing that kind of thing—that paradoxical purpose-building, that sometimes-befuddling streak of originality.

GOD'S GREATER PURPOSE

The guy had always had a serious speech impediment, and time hadn't helped resolve it. As a kid, he'd done well in school and was considered quite bright. He'd excelled in all his courses and was athletic and smart. But his speech issues had always made him somewhat doubtful and unsure when it came to high-level negotiations and public speaking.

After an unfortunate run-in with the law as a younger man, he'd decided to pursue a more rural life, going into ranching. Life was moving at a predictable pace until one day he was approached with a singularly profound opportunity, a truly once-in-a-lifetime offer. His curious threads of intelligence, loyalty, and attractive persona should have made his acceptance of this offer immediate. But his perceived weakness in communicating made him wary about taking the offer. And assurances that he'd be equipped with a variety of negotiating tools weren't enough to calm his concern. His speech impediment had made any idea of being a public communicator seem impossible. And at some point, it became difficult to discern if his speech impediment was the real reason for his hesitancy—or if he more broadly lacked the confidence to take on such a position of influence.

With lots of coaxing and reassurance, he finally entered into the diplomatic arena of an era, the weakness of his speech and the strength of God in full array.

Moses had become the voice of a nation.

A dropped stitch.

A greater purpose.

THE VIEW

It hadn't been evident immediately. As an infant, all had seemed well. The baby nursed. He babbled. He grinned. He grew. He started to roll over. He sat up.

But the day came when his parents realized their baby's beautiful brown eyes, rich in color and fringed with generous lashes, received no light, no shape, no visual information. And their world shifted and tilted. They tried to fix it, tried to fix him. The neighbors gave their advice. The village healer chimed in. Herbs were mixed, ideas were blended, cures were suggested. All to no avail.

He was blind.

Because of the place and time in which he lived, he was looked upon by his community with suspicious pity. With a driblet of unease. With a splash of aversion. The emotional antidotes to a condition that trafficked on a human fear.

The fear of not being able to see.

Not being able to behold the face of a loved one. Not being able to see the path. Not being able to watch the sunrise, view the vista, drink in the color.

The years passed. He took up the one profession available to him in that place and time. He sat along the roadway. He crouched in the dust. He extended his hand.

He begged.

One day a teacher came walking along the blind beggar's road, a group of his students with him. They encountered the man working his corner, engaged in his trade of supplication. The students kicked up some familiar philosophical questions.

Why was this guy born blind? Who is at fault? Him? His parents? What was the sin that resulted in this condition?

They voiced things often wondered at when life gives you glimpses of the difficult, the challenging, the perceived weaknesses.

Let's settle it, their questions say. *Let's place the blame. Name the sin. Learn how to avoid this difficulty, this inconvenience, this nuisance to clean lines and tidy theology.*

The teacher had just come from an interesting encounter—an assassination attempt. Some guys from his local church were ready to take him out, but he slipped away, hidden from their fury. As he was walking along his escape route, the blind beggar came into view. And this is the point where the teacher's students want to doctor doctrine. They pitch their questions regarding causality and sin and culpability.

The teacher doesn't say much.

But he says everything.

"Neither this man nor his parents sinned . . . but this happened so that the works of God might be displayed in him" (John 9:3).

The teacher, Jesus, goes on to heal the blind man, much to the anger of the religious, the rule followers, the niche keepers. They haul in the blind man's parents, demand the medical records, do a personal identity check. They question him, accuse him, and attempt to put him back where they think he belongs—the unseeing guy by the side of the road.

But it's too late. The power of God has been displayed in his life. He now sees more clearly than the religious of the day, not just an ophthalmological clarity but a clarity of the deepest, most high-definition sort.

He sees the power of God in his life.

A dropped stitch.

A greater purpose.

THE LOVER

The guy was a lover. His curious thread of passion was a gorgeous strand to behold, weaving joyous abandon and ardent song into the artistry of his life.

He was a lover *and* a fighter, with a thread of passion that found its weaving in his military and political career—passionately fearless, passionately driven, passionately focused. He won battles no one thought he could win. He took risks no one else took. The feverous strand that stood most evident in his personality gleamed with courage and leadership, a string held taut and ready on a bow of destiny.

But lest we get too comfortable with our personal strengths, we need to realize the risk that is present.

This guy's powerful strength carried great risk—a risk that was realized at the height of his popularity, fame, and influence. His zeal for living a legendary life, for passionately throwing himself into the full banquet of possibility, sped past his seatbelt of righteousness. He careened headlong into an extramarital affair and contracted a hit on his lover's husband. The very strength that had carried him to the heights of accomplishment now crushed members of his family and compromised his reputation. Most importantly, his hidden guilt created a distance between himself and the God he loved so passionately. One of his strongest threads had become a snare.

King David learned a difficult lesson. Our greatest strengths can become our greatest weaknesses. That beautiful thread of diligence becomes a weakness if we elevate tasks over people. That gorgeous string of ingenuity can veer into a chasm of selfish artistry, where creativity trumps relationships and commitments. That exquisite twine of loyalty can twist into a weakness of pleasing people instead of pleasing God.

We should never become more dependent on the gifting than on the Giver.

THE MUSCLE

Prior to his birth, his mother had settled into a life of childlessness, her sterility a popular topic of conversation among the locals. She and her husband had become accustomed to their quiet existence. The days and years clicked by with calm consistency.

Until one day.

An angel shows up. Announces to her that she will conceive. Admonishes her to give up that late afternoon glass of wine. Asks her to get used to long hair on a boy, because that's going to be part of the deal.

What the angel foretells happens. A baby boy is born. He grows, and he grows some more. He takes down a lion barehanded. Engages an enemy nation. He's a brawler—a brawny, singular specimen of a man. By power of might and mind, he begins to bring the Philistine nation to its knees.

But that amazing strength has its fragile places. He doesn't withhold much from his muscular body when it comes to women. And he doesn't withhold much from his muscular will when it comes to emotion. He's angry, arrogant, and amorous. His enemies became more strategic. They barter with his latest girlfriend, anxious to subvert his curious threads of strength. She needles him, begs him, wheedles him to reveal his secret. He tells her new ropes will bind him. They snap like threads. He tells her to weave his hair into a loom, the seven braids of his hair rendered into a fabric piece. It's all a ruse. All it takes is a razor to scrape away the threads of his vow, his Nazarite tresses of uncut hair, to return him to a point of origin, a creature dependent on God. It is there that he finds his true strength.

Samson, eyes now gouged out by his enemies and strength now fully given over to God, took out more of Israel's enemies broken than he did whole.

A dropped stitch.

A greater purpose.

Moses had a speech impediment—and he became the voice of a nation.

Abraham was infertile—and he became the father of nations.

David's curious thread of strong passion led to his greatest fall—yet that thread was also the mainstay of his passion for God.

Samson's great strand of strength began the deliverance of Israel from the hand of the Philistines—but only after his dependence on God was established through weakness.

Paul had trouble with his eyes—and he became the vision caster for the redemption of the Gentiles as well as the catalyst for worldwide missions.

Curiously, in Kingdom parenting, God often chooses to use the thing we think is frailest to reveal purpose and His great strength.

Some might say that my daughter Maesyn's fragility is that she's hearing impaired. I say it's a God strength, that miraculous place where He takes what the world classifies as not enough and reconfigures it in His power. Because Maesyn has hearing loss, she needs to listen carefully, intentionally. And so her strength is that she's a powerful listener. People naturally gravitate toward her because she listens so intently. She's also a remarkably bold speaker of truth—possibly the strongest evangelist of our tribe, always at the ready to discuss faith and her relationship with the Lord. She's had to labor to acquire words, to master language, and so she's all the more potent in her communication.

As British missionary to China James Hudson Taylor wrote, "All God's giants have been weak men who did great things for God because they reckoned on God being with them."

MORAL FAILURE OR TEMPERAMENT NATURE?

Let's get something straight here.

Being shy is not a sin.

Feeling more comfortable completing tasks than chatting it up with people is not ethically wrong.

Tending to be disorganized isn't immoral.

Struggling with change isn't a crime.

Those traits may or may not be our preferences. They may not be convenient. They may need to be coached so that basics of life—like balancing a checkbook and getting along with coworkers—can be easier.

But they aren't sin.

Pride is sin.

Self-reliance is sin.

Taking credit and glory away from God is sin.

Going one's own way apart from the direction of God is sin.

Elevating fear over faith is sin.

Sin crosses all personality styles, potentially polluting gifting, talents, and abilities. It can take advantage of the insecurities and issues in our personality styles. And it can particularly exploit those areas where we think we're strongest, those substantial strands of talent and passion and focus. As parents, what we sometimes perceive as sin and transgression has far more to do with the world's standards than with God's truth. We don't like that our son is hesitant. We resent that our daughter is embarrassingly energetic. We begrudge that our offspring are messy and forgetful. And we elevate those traits to sin, responding and reacting as if moral code has been shattered.

Conversely, if we have a kid who's getting elected to student council or excelling on the athletic field, we can overlook a self-involved attitude, a haughtiness of spirit, or a chronic lack of respect. Our kid's strengths can blind us to the quicksand of epic ego. When we only give feedback on accomplishment and allow character and kindness to slide, we're sending a direct message that the means to the end don't matter, that integrity can be ignored if the results make our kid—and us—look good.

In my children's experiences in sports, theater, and dance, it's been remarkable to see kids who are all kinds of awful when it comes to attitude be celebrated because of their skill in a certain area. Let's face it—in a fallen world, the instruments of sin can and do work. A teen athlete who verbally abuses his competitors, a performer who boasts a high level of self-involvement, a student who lives on stress and smarts and insolence—we call it competitive spirit, we call it confidence, we call it being all-in. We reward it. And we see it rewarded in the family of God as well.

But it's sin.

Now, I'm not talking about having confidence and a can-do spirit—not when it's a God-confidence and a God-can-do spirit. God said to Joshua, the successor to Moses, "Be strong and courageous. . . . Be strong and *very* courageous . . . that you may be successful wherever you go" (Joshua 1:7, emphasis added). God goes on to say it a third time in the same passage, a trio of repeated charge. And Joshua does it. He is incredibly strong and courageous. He grabs destiny and leadership by the horns. He's decisive, bold, authoritative. And what God accomplishes through him is stunning. Jericho falls. Time is bent. Enemies are vanquished left, right, center, north, south, east, and west. Joshua cleans house. Sets up processes for land inhabitance. Fully claims the promised land. His strengths, talents, and abilities are many, but they all solidly abide in their obedience to God, in accomplishing His purposes.

No, what I'm talking about here are the star performers who are allowed to bully and pout and rant, simply because they have gifts our culture admires. Let's not be afraid to call sin a sin when necessary, even with those whose talent and confidence are powerful. Let's not call our preferences for personality and accomplishment a virtue and anything short of those preferences a sin. The boundaries of righteousness are firm, but the room within the kingdom of God for personality and sparkle and expression gives gracious elbow room.

Just like our strands of DNA, just like Zélie's lace, there is always room for individuality, imagination, and originality within the borders of grace and in the weaving of our kids. Integrity, compassion, honesty, and sincerity make for a strong hem around a life, but within the field of that border is room for expression, creativity, and an individual flourish. Space to breathe. Space to grow. Space to find voice.

"In a very real sense not one of us is qualified, but it seems that God continually chooses the most unqualified to do his work, to bear his glory," Madeline L'Engle writes in *Walking on Water: Reflections on Faith and Art*. "If we are qualified, we tend to think that we have done the job ourselves. If we are forced to accept our evident lack of qualification, then there's no danger that we will confuse God's work with our own, or God's glory with our own."

In the weaving of originality, strength and weakness, fullness and space, power and frailty all have their place in the fabric. Sometimes, the very things we see as a lack are the very places where God shows up in the richness of His purpose. In coaching our kids to walk in their destinies,

> **AND THEN THERE'S THIS: GOD HASN'T ASKED US TO RAISE PERFECT CHILDREN. HE'S ASKED US TO RAISE PURPOSED CHILDREN.**

let's make sure we not only point out their fortes but also their fragilities as exciting markers for where God just may be up to something profound. And then there's this: God hasn't asked us to raise perfect children. He's asked us to raise purposed children. Let's elevate divine purpose over human definitions of perfection.

CHAPTER 11

ORIGINALS GIVEN BACK TO THE ORIGINATOR

*Nothing that you have not given
away will ever truly be yours.*

C. S. Lewis

GREAT.

Now the priest thought she was a hysterical drunk.

As if it wasn't enough that Hannah was already dealing with a contentious, hyper-procreative sister-wife who jabbed her at every turn, taunting the taut line of Hannah's flat stomach while pushing out the curve of her own globular belly. Another baby for Peninnah, another empty ache for Hannah.

Not to mention Elkanah—Hannah's husband. And Peninnah's husband. *Their* husband. Who is tired of the competition for conception between his two wives—Peninnah's preening pride versus Hannah's hurt humiliation. Elkanah's solution is to offer Hannah extra food, the only thing he knows to do. Hannah is confident she has her husband's heart, but she does not have his heir. And so it goes—the cruelty of Peninnah, the clueless helplessness of Elkanah, and a longing in her heart that finds no ease.

And now this.

The three of them have made their journey to Shiloh, the location of the Tent of Meeting and the home of the Ark of the Covenant. It's as close as Hannah can imagine being to God, His presence reported to be centered between the cherubim on either side of the Ark's lid. She'd been here before, year after year. Peninnah has antagonized her year after year, as the time at the Tent seems to be impotent for Hannah, her womb still desolate, her hope still dismayed. Yet here they are again—Hannah weeping, Peninnah smug, Elkanah bewildered. It's almost time to leave, to make the trek back to Ramathaim, to return to the bleakness of daily routine. Hannah makes for the Tent of Meeting, stopping outside its walls of tapestry. She weeps. She prays. She pleads silently, lips moving, voice muted.

One desperate word after another. All the contents of her heart spilling inaudibly, splashing silently before the throne of God. She promises. She assures. She tells God that if He'll grant her a son, she'll do the one thing that would seem most unfathomable after having waited so long for a baby. She'll give that son back to God, to serve Him always.

It is the only altar available to her, the only sacrifice worthy of such an anguished request.

And now the priest—corpulent, laggard Eli, rumors of his wild sons swirling around his hulking frame, splayed in a chair leaned against the doorpost of the Tent—begins chastising her for her deepest expression of prayer, that kind of prayer so deep, so sacred, that form and convention fall away and a soul stands bare.

That kind of prayer.

Eli accuses Hannah of being drunk.

Drunk, in her moment of greatest clarity.

He tells Hannah to put down the wine. To straighten up. Sober up. Calm down.

I have some things I would have liked to say to Eli—things that would have involved telling him to put down the fried chicken and get his two skirt-chasing boys under control.

That's not what Hannah said.

Hannah. Sweet Hannah.

With respect and kindness, she tells Eli she hasn't been getting into the cooking wine, that she is instead staggered with grief, with anguish, and that she's spilling every essence of her very marrow into this conversation with the Lord.

And so Eli speaks blessing over her, words of peace, telling her he hopes God grants what she has asked.

Between her time in prayer and her interaction with Eli, Hannah finds a thread of hope. It's enough to lift her eyes as she makes the long trek back to Ramathaim. It's enough to awaken her appetite. To brighten her mood.

Eli doesn't see Hannah again for a few years. Elkanah and Peninnah make the trip to Shiloh the following year. And the next. Hannah isn't with them. I wonder if Hannah ever crossed Eli's mind, if he ever wondered what had become of the young woman he'd been certain was drinking midday. Or if he ever wondered what her request to the Lord had been.

The time comes again for Elkanah to make his sacrifice at Shiloh, but this time Hannah returns, holding the lead for a three-year-old bull in one hand, the small hand of her son clasped in the other. The bull is sacrificed, a measure of flour and a flask of wine are given, and then Hannah approaches Eli with the most precious gift she's ever received. She takes her son's small hand and places it in Eli's. "As surely as you live," she says to the old priest, "I am the woman who stood here beside you praying to the Lord. I prayed for this child, and the Lord has granted me what I asked of him. So now I give him to the Lord. For his whole life he will be given over to the Lord" (1 Samuel 1:26–28).

OUR KIDS BELONG TO GOD

It staggers me, really.

This handing off of Samuel, the longed-for son of Hannah, to the priest Eli. Hannah had waited until her son was weaned before she brought him to Shiloh, but even if Samuel nursed longer than our Western conventions, he was still a young child. And she brings him to Eli.

Eli.

Not Dr. James Dobson. Not Mr. Rogers. Not Dr. Benjamin Spock. *Eli.* Eli with the serious overeating issues. Eli whose track record raising kids is not stellar. At all.

Eli's sons are serving as priests at the Tent of Meeting, and they've got their hands in the cookie jar. They skim off the best offerings. They sleep with the women who come to serve at church. And Eli? He's old—as in, very old. As in, won't-be-able-to-toss-a-baseball-in-the-yard old.

This is the person to whom Hannah hands off her son.

I think I would have found reason—any reason—to hedge the vow, to tell God I'd make good on my promise and all, but the situation needed to be better, the players of higher quality, the season of life a bit more stable.

Hannah doesn't.

She makes good on what she said she'd do. Because she's not focused on Eli. She's focused on her son serving God for a lifetime.

When I read her story, it's tempting to think of it as an exotic circumstance, an extraordinary occurrence. *Whew,* I think. *Giving kids back over to the service of the Lord—our wild, untamable, mysterious God. Glad it's sort of a once-in-a-millennium moment.* Or, *There, there. It's just a cultural thing.* Because when Hannah gives her firstborn son in service to God, she's not just keeping the promise she made to the Lord. She's also fulfilling what had been a longtime custom of the Jews. In the book of Numbers, God had commanded that all the firstborn males—from humans of the tribe of Levi to livestock—were to be given to God. God had specified those particular firstborns because the Levites were to serve him as priests. Elkanah, husband of Hannah and father of Samuel, is of the Levite tribe as recorded in 1 Chronicles 6:34, which means that Samuel is a Levite as well. *See,* I think. *It's because of the whole priest-tribe connection.*

Except it's not.

It's not the exemption to me dedicating my kids to God.

Not when I go digging into Scripture to prove my point and come out with another side proven.

Abraham gets to make a potentially propitiatory field trip with Isaac, right up to the point of putting Isaac on the altar and drawing the knife. Abraham understandably, after so long without an heir, could have been at risk for seeing Isaac as his legacy, as the center of his future. But God dramatically reminds him that He must be first and symbolically shows Abraham that his identity, his self-concept, his faithfulness to God, can't be supplanted by this promised child. Yes, God miraculously brought Isaac into Abraham and Sarah's lives. But Abraham's ultimate hope and trust must abide in God, not in the life of his son.

Jocabed, birth mother of Moses, must allow Moses to ride down the waters of the Nile before arriving at his destiny in God. Elizabeth and Zechariah know prior to the positive pregnancy test that the baby she would one day carry had a specific mission to fulfill. Paul says he was set apart even before birth for the role he was to play in taking the gospel to the Gentiles.

I have plenty of postulations, hunches, and quantum questions about how the interplay of God's omniscience and our free will coexist cooperatively, and I'm sure the way it all works is far beyond my mental gymnastics. But I do know that many of the compelling stories lived out in the pages of the Bible required a giving over of self and an awakening of belonging to God. And the parents we read about in the Bible—those who were entrusted with these babies who would go on to lead nations, change the world, write powerful letters, and carve a new chapter for humanity—cooperated in the giving back to God the children entrusted to them.

And this.

Because of Jesus, we are now a priesthood. All of us. No more rigid family lines marking those dedicated to God's service and those who fall outside the line. No more leaving ministry up to a select few. No more trying to grasp at strands of self-determination over selfless dedication. "As you come to him, the living Stone—rejected by humans but chosen by God and precious to him—you also, like living stones, are being built into a spiritual house to be a holy priesthood, offering spiritual sacrifices acceptable to God through Jesus Christ," writes that brawling fisherman apostle Peter (1 Peter 2:4–5).

Life with Jesus implies a life dedicated to the priesthood of His ministry, a life called to do His will. For all of us. Including those kids we are raising.

Originals given back to the Originator.

UNSPEAKABLY PROFOUND

As I mentioned in chapter 9, one of my best friends, Jessica—also my running partner, three-doors-down neighbor, and keeper of my sanity—and her husband adopted a little boy from Ethiopia in 2011. Our whole crew was immediately smitten with Jonathan—his huge personality, his wide smile, his raucous laugh. Having him show up in our lives from half a world away, along with all the details of how he came to us, was simply an exquisite wonderment to me. For the first several months he was home, I cried almost every time I was with him. We knew lots of families who had adopted and had seriously considered adoption ourselves. But there was something about Jonathan, about his placement in our lives, that was at first an untranslatable epiphany. In those early days with him, I was consistently overwhelmed, aware I was standing on holy ground but unable to read the contours of the experience. I was like a crazed grandparent, constantly sharing the pictures I had of Jonathan on my phone and tearing up whenever I talked about him.

And then one day, I understood. I had the translation. God deciphered what I was experiencing, the response of my uncustomary tears.

The profundity that Jonathan would overcome so many obstacles, such crazy probability factors, across a continent and an ocean to live life with us in this time and place is no more and no less a miracle than the obstacles and crazy probability factors that Jonathan's adoptive siblings overcame. No more and no less a miracle than the appearance of my children and yours. Adoptive or biological, we have only a one in four hundred trillion "chance" of our conception occurring when it does. The fact that any of us singularly show up on the planet when we do, where we do, is against all odds. Regardless of how we arrived at this time and place, that fact that each of us is here—right in this moment—is unspeakably profound.

With Jonathan, I'd been given a fresh glimpse of how sacred it is that any of us are sharing this planet at the same time. That any of us are sharing the same community. That any of us are sharing the same home. That any of us are sharing the same moment. The more extreme aspects of Jonathan's arrival heightened my awareness of that sacredness. And inherent in the word *sacred* is the word *sacrifice*. Born of the same root word—*sacrare* in the Old

Latin—meaning to set apart, to dedicate, to make holy, to anoint. All of us arrive with some element of sacrifice in the mix, some more dramatic than others, but a sacrifice made—a consecration, a setting apart from the start.

In light of Hannah's story, I can't help but think back to what we read about Jephthah in chapter 6. From a vague view, both Hannah and Jephthah asked God for something. Both offered something in return. And both followed through, even when it meant giving their children over to God. But Hannah makes her deal with God from a place of wanting to serve Him. Jephthah's deal comes from a place of serving his own motives. And that's what I need to search in my own heart. One way or another, our children already belong to the Lord. Whose motives am I trying to accomplish? God's, or my own misguided ideas for my life story? Hannah and Jephthah both hand their children over to God, but Hannah's sacrifice is for the purpose of dedicating Samuel to the Lord's service. Jephthah's sacrifice becomes a sacrilege, because he has stolen what is consecrated to God—the life of his daughter—and used it for his own purposes.

A sacred sacrifice or a sacrilege?

It's a holy balance, to take responsibility for the loving and raising of our children, doing it with excellence, and simultaneously cupping their lives gently and protectively in an open hand.

TAKE CARE

Scripture tells us that Hannah would visit Samuel every year. And there's a little side note that I find fascinating. First Samuel 2:18–20 says that Samuel would minister before the Lord and that he would wear a linen ephod. An ephod was a piece of clothing worn by those who were priests of the Lord. God had given instructions for the design and wearing of ephods when He brought His people out of Egypt and had them build the Tabernacle. And here was Samuel, already wearing a pint-size uniform in keeping with God's call on his life.

There's also something else that Samuel wore. Each year when Hannah came to visit, she would bring a little coat she'd made for him. Each year she would outfit him afresh in a new garment. I love that Hannah did this every year. I imagine her sewing each stitch into the linen, estimating how much her son had grown in the months since she'd last seen him. She had to take care not to make the robe too big or it would have tripped up the boy. And she had to take care not to make it too small, as that would have hindered him. It took observation, patience, and care on Hannah's part. It took seeing Samuel as he really was, not bigger or more mature than his current season. And not younger or smaller either. There's something so right, so poetic, in Samuel wearing both the garment of the priesthood's call on his life while also wearing the garment of his mother's love, guidance, and sacrifice.

We need to take the same care in the coats of expectation we stitch for our own children. When we saddle them with expectations that are too heavy, they can wilt beneath the weight. But when we constrict them with a vision that is too small, we can stunt their spiritual growth. We must always make careful measurement of exactly who they are, of who God has made them to be.

As believing parents, most of us would say we want our kids to serve God. But that phrase can vary in vagueness. Or it can constrict in assumption. Sometimes families who have a long history of vocational ministry can place that heavy mantle on the slim shoulders of a child, only allowing for a narrow definition of serving God. Conversely, we can sometimes steer a young person away from the challenges of living life as an overseas missionary or patching together a path that concurrently requires working early mornings at the corner coffee shop while serving as the part-time youth pastor in a fledgling church community. We want them to serve God, but we don't want it to be tough or inconvenient. We don't want to turn them over to Eli, so to speak. But if we aren't earnestly observing the work of God in our child's life, we might be making a coat that is too overwhelming or too constricting for them.

THE CHOREOGRAPHIC COMBINATION

Michael and I love new ventures. We love to equip people to find ways out of a lifestyle that isn't working. We love to dream up new business ideas. We love to problem solve and dream big and explore new territories. And we've worked to instill those characteristics and values in our kids as well.

Which sometimes may have worked a little too well.

Because we've never wanted our kids to feel trapped in an unrewarding situation or a job that wasn't working or a circumstance that had gone stagnant, we've long promoted to them the idea that they can change their environment, adjust their thinking, rise higher, and set their own course. We encouraged them to be goal setters. Problem solvers. Thought influencers. All very noble, all very proactive. Good, grand stuff. But when one child was wrestling with carefully crafted plans that hadn't unfolded the way they'd been strategized, I realized afresh the importance of that ancient choreography, that delicate dance of our own goals and God's mysteries. All that well-intentioned training in goal setting and vision casting had not shown the variables of that dance as clearly as it should have. And so as a reminder to both myself and my kids, I printed out a verse that explains the choreographic combination:

In their hearts humans plan their course,
but the LORD establishes their steps.

Proverbs 16:9

This verse lives in a frame in our home, immediately visible during the dance of our days. It's not enough for me to give my kids over to God. They also need to give themselves over to Him. They need to understand: that's part of the Christian walk. And it's up to me to communicate that truth and then to live it out before them. It's another instance where knowing my children's original personalities helps me to guide them. For a child with a Director or Curator personality, the idea of giving over their plans, their goals, their checklists, to an invisible God can act as direct friction to their preference for control. For the Inspirer and the Steadfast, it takes awareness on their part to understand that they could be at risk of allowing public opinion or affection to win out over being dedicated to God.

Any number of factors—our preferences, our fears, our fascinations—can make us pull back from being fully devoted to God. A life dedicated to God takes more than immersion in the waters of baptism, participation in communion, fellowship on Sunday mornings. Those things can symbolize and assist our walks of faith, but yielding to God takes practice. It takes putting ourselves into His arms. It takes leaning into His lead. We may get to plan the party and pick the music, but God will establish the steps.

Céline Martin, one of Zélie the lacemaker's five daughters, wrote a biography of her mother's life called *The Mother of the Little Flower*. She penned the family moments, the funny and the sad, the morsels of wisdom and love that were dispensed throughout her childhood in her parents' home. She noted that Zélie was intentional in weaving into the dialog of their home life a dedicating of one's days to God. "Mother," she wrote, "took an active part in our education. I recollect how she always made us say our morning and evening prayers and taught us the following formula for the offering of the day: My God, I give You my heart; please accept it that no creature, but You alone, my good Jesus, may possess it."[15]

May we help weave these words, such an homage to the message spoken by Hannah and intended for Samuel, into the songs of our families.

PRAYING HANNAH'S PRAYER

Now, you had to know this was coming, that I would ask you to take this step. And you may resist and twist and squirm. But we're going to try, you and I. We're going to link arms with our sister Hannah and walk through how to pray her prayer and mean it. And you're going to need some courage. It may take a couple of tries. Or four. Or more. It may be a daily discipline of giving over. But we're going to do it. Because we love our kids that much. We love them more than ourselves, more than our agendas, more than our fears. In our most honest moments, we know that all the machinations, all our notions of control, are ludicrous. And that even more than we love our kids, we love God.

God, we're putting You first again.

Father, in the most vulnerable places of our hearts—those expanses where You have called us to be parents—we've made the terrain of that field what is most dominant at times. We've made the desire for children, the complexities of raising children, the dreams we place on our children, more apparent, more loved, more worshipped than You. Forgive us, Abba.

You reign, Lord. You reign in our hearts, in our attention, in what comes first.

You are first.

God, we're trusting You.

And it's hard. The world is scary. The world is dangerous. And our hearts are so very fragile. What if You do things differently than we would? What if You allow something to happen that we just can't understand? What if Your call upon our children's lives is something far bigger than we could imagine and completely unknown to anything in our experience? What if You call them to the world stage? What if You call them to obscurity? What if You call them to mediocre grades and a tender heart? What if Your idea of success doesn't look like our diploma'ed Western expectation? What if they struggle?

Lord, here's the whole soggy bundle. Our "what-ifs." Which spell fear. Which, defined, is not trusting You.

Father, we trust You.

God, we're giving these children over to serve You.

Our hearts are in our throats, Lord. We've called them "our" kids for so long, when all along they've belonged to You. More than the hopes and dreams we've poured into them, You've seeded destiny. May we never interfere with what You're up to.

We want to guide them, Lord, toward You, toward the plans You have for them. We want to honor exactly who they are, who You have knit them to be. Help us transition from exerting ownership over our kids to understanding that You have graciously extended to us an invitation through our kids to participate with You in ubiquity. Life without end. Creation without constraint.

So here it goes, Lord. Here it goes—with all our fears and dreams and selfishness and identity crises and issues, the good and the bad, the positive and the negative.

Lord, these children, these babies You've placed in our lives— we give them over to You, to serve You all of their days.

Amen.

Rinse and repeat as necessary.

PART 5

THE LAUNCH

CHAPTER 12

AN ORIGINAL LEGACY

Be happy every day. Don't be boastful. Do things now.

Bob Lyles

A BEAUTIFUL PIECE of completed lace is a celebration of curious threads spun in a unique pattern. It's a triumph not only of where the threads have been placed but also in the space between those threads, a dance of what has been added and removed. Thread and space. Designer and drafter.

As lacemakers, we help weave our children's lives. We seek their curious threads. We encourage. We modify. We strengthen their "Knots." We teach them how to manage their "Nots." We plant deep roots of integrity and compassion. We nurture the soil of their environment. We prune. We water. We pray.

And then we launch them.

We move from lacemakers . . .

. . . to launchers.

From planters . . .

. . . to propellers.

During the heyday of lace, one of its prized features was that it could be taken off one garment and attached to another. It could become an heirloom, a treasure, a gift of artistry and time to be enjoyed by the next generation.

Now, about this business of handing off to the next generation. What will be that indelible mark of us? It's not something we weave for our own sakes. It's not our own identity that we should stamp so deeply on our children that they never realize their own. Instead, it's like Fred Rogers said in the quote that kicked off the first chapter of this book: "Parents are like shuttles on a loom. They join the threads of the past with threads of the future and leave their own bright patterns as they go."

In our generation of innovation, technology, and a tidal wave of new, the concept of legacy has become a quaint relic. We're so busy, so scheduled, so distracted, that time ticks, the clock shifts, and we fail to be intentional about what it is exactly that we want to impart to our kids.

What do we want our kids to know—really know, to the core—when they launch?

And the launch is the goal, right?

When I began working on this chapter, the passing of days was very much in my focus.

My daddy had died twenty-two days before.

Twenty-two days.

That felt like years.

That felt like seconds.

That didn't feel real.

And all too real.

Depending on the moment.

Moments.

The moments that comprised those twenty-two days.

The perfume of legacy and heartache and sweet memory and

loss swirled and scented the air. It flickered across every glance of my soul with its solemnly paced questions of purpose and urgency and lessons and priorities.

His absence so very present.

A mist of missing him, the mist that was his life.

And the mist that is allotted to me, the time given me to tell my story. Am I doing that—am I being intentional, am I making sure I'm pouring out all I've got to give?

What have I done with my curious threads?

What are you doing with yours?

Are we weaving something with our lives that can be passed on to the next generation?

A LASTING LEGACY

For about ten years, Elijah mentored and taught and helped develop Elisha as a future leader. A dramatic and powerful prophet, Elijah had called down rain from heaven, struggled through episodes of depression, enjoyed seasons of intense acclaim, and confronted rumors of potential assassination. During a particularly challenging time of triumph and threat, God told Elijah to go find and anoint Elisha. He told Elijah that Elisha would help bring to justice those who had broken the covenant of God. Elijah went and found Elisha driving the tractor of the day, a plow running on twelve-oxen horsepower. First Kings 19:19 says that Elijah went up to Elisha and threw his cloak around the younger man, signifying a farm-side anointing, a symbolic gesture that Elisha would be groomed to wear Elijah's mantle—an extension of the purpose and reach of the prophet.

For the next decade, Elisha served Elijah as an attendant, soaking up the lessons and legacies of the seasoned prophet. Evil monarchies were overturned, sin was chased into the daylight, repentance was demanded. Politics and prophecy, leadership and lineage, Elijah fought to the end for the restoration of righteousness of the nation of Israel. And Elisha watched and learned and absorbed. Elijah's vivid and theatrical personality and Elisha's steadier, more measured temperament found their weaving in the larger canvas of Israel's history and God's will.

Elijah's cloak showed up again in the narrative of Elisha's apprenticeship with him. God told Elijah, Elisha, and fifty other prophets that Elijah would be taken from them. The day had been circled on the calendar. The fifty other prophets watched from a distance, but Elisha stayed with Elijah to the end. Elijah and Elisha made their way to the banks of the Jordan, and Elijah took off that cloak once more, this time to strike the waters of the river and create a crossing of dry ground for himself and his faithful intern. In a final conversation, Elijah turned to his protégé, his child in the Spirit, and asked if there was anything he could do for Elisha before being taken. Elisha asked for a double portion of Elijah's spirit.

Not the deed to the land.

Not the access code to the savings account.

Not the heirloom china.

But an inheritance of spirit and devotion and calling and purpose.

Legacy.

Elisha saw Elijah taken up in a whirlwind, a chariot of fire finally splitting the fabric of time between the two men. Elisha marveled at the transformation he witnessed, grieved the leave-taking of his spiritual father, and turned to go.

And there was the cloak of Elijah, lying right where it had fallen in the midst of the rapturous wind and inferno.

Elisha picked up the cloak. He used it once again to part the waters of the Jordan. And he strode into a new day, one in which he continued to carry on the purpose of God, the mantle of holy heritage about his shoulders, carving his own original story, doubly blessed.

THE BLUE SHIRT

When Michael married me, he discovered that I often slept in a cloak, so to speak—an oversized blue dress shirt.

A blue dress shirt that had once belonged to my dad.

Blue dress shirts.

They were my dad's calling card—symbols of where he'd started and where he'd arrived. From his Mississippi roots, he'd literally reached for the stars. His career was crafted from a blend of dreaming and engineering, his goal to build motors and systems that would allow men to fly into space. The stuff of fantasy built on Fibonacci numbers.

And his uniform for playing in the possibilities of the galaxy?

Blue dress shirts.

His blue dress shirts were part of my first entrepreneurial efforts. I subcontracted myself out to iron those shirts. He paid me ten cents per shirt—a dime a dress shirt. It now dawns on me that there may have been some child labor laws that were in questionable keeping.

When I left for college, I packed a couple of his castoff shirts, ones with collars that were no longer fashionable or cuffs that were frayed. The watery blue one with long tails became "the one"—my late-night studying garb, my comfort attire. And that didn't change even after my engagement and marriage. Or even through my first labor and delivery.

It was this blue shirt that I wore as I labored with my first baby. It was a buffer of comfort and contact through a long and painful day . . . and night . . . and day. As time went on, the blue shirt became my painting shirt, my project shirt, my stain-the-deck shirt, my knock-down-a-wall shirt.

It acquired some rips and stains. It became more precious.

It was a constant point of contact with my daddy. I began to realize it had become my uniform for studying, for delving into DIY projects, for having the courage to push through labor pains, for simply hanging out on a lazy weekend. Creation and rest. Projects and curiosity. The construct of worn cloth an unconscious beacon keeping me linked to the lessons my dad taught me, both spoken and unspoken.

And then it dawned on me.

For all its symbolism and meaning, I've now actually owned this shirt longer than my dad did. He wore it for a handful of years. I've worn it for thirty. It's been mine longer than it was his.

But that was always his goal for me.

He gave me life. He raised me with tremendous influence, strict guidance, high expectations. I lived in his home for seventeen years before I departed for college, and he was integral to every facet of those years—guiding, molding, worrying.

And then he launched me.

And let me fly.

He handed off the shirt of his experiences and his hopes and his story and let me take ownership for what happened next. He was always there for me but didn't believe in rescuing me. He knew I would figure it out. And so I did.

In telling his story, I often focus on the fact that he helped put people into space, that he played not in a box of sand but a box of stardust. In retrospect, though, I don't think that was the point.

I think his driving passion was the launch. The takeoff. The runway. Getting enough heart and momentum and encouragement behind an idea, behind a person, behind a dream, that the entity could become a vehicle for reaching so much farther than before.

To say he was a rocket scientist isn't quite right.

He was a launch scientist—a keen observer of ideas and invention and vision and what it would take to get those ideas and dreams off the ground.

After he slipped from the chains of time into timelessness, from the sterile confines of the ICU, I went back to my parents' house, shell-shocked, exhausted, eyes burning. I found myself wandering into his bedroom and just stood there, heart aching. His bookshelves were still filled with binders of plans and ideas. His desk was still stacked with notes and figures. His computer was still a labyrinth of research and possibility. His pictures and models of rockets and the Shuttle still adorned the room. *There was so much he wanted to do,* I thought. *So many ideas yet to be realized that he didn't get to finish.*

But my perspective was the wrong one.

In the Bible, King David determined that he'd be the one who would build a temple to the Lord. He made all kinds of plans for all the right reasons and was headlong into the project when the Lord revealed to him that, in fact, he would not be the one to complete the project. It would be his son, Solomon. With this news, David could have traveled to a place of regret, a place of resentment. Instead, he became a launch scientist.

He carefully gathered all the materials and resources Solomon would need for the project and made sure his son would have access to helpful information and intelligent advisors. Best of all, he never begrudged the fact that it would be the next generation to realize his dreams and vision.

David focused on the launch sequence. He built the runaway. He allowed the next generation to fly.

And that's what my dad did. It's his legacy to me. His physical body simply couldn't contain all the vision and ingenuity of his drive. But what he gathered and stored and categorized is all there—a treasure trove of wisdom that will allow the next generation and the next and the next to build and care and make a difference and live even more fully in their originality.

So I'll continue to wear my blue dress shirt.

I'll make something of what he gathered.

PREPARING FOR THE LAUNCH

There's an age—usually around four or five, it seems—when each of my children has declared they will live with their daddy and me when they grow up. That they'll just stay and make sure we're not lonely. That they'll just, you know, continue to hang out with us. For our good, of course. Not because their world has begun to expand and they're beginning to see that growing up is a little more complicated than they thought.

Of course.

I have to smile when those conversations come my way. Because while I do think it would be pretty cool to have some acreage and stick a few houses on it and have my kids living within a short jog's distance, there will come a time when they'll want to be on their own. When *we* want them to be on their own.

Michael and I have some plans, you know.

We did things a little backwards. We had our first baby fifteen months into our marriage. We skipped that period of time when we could have traveled and made some memories, just the two of us.

That's not any kind of regret thing.

We just hope to have some time at the other end of this parenting journey to get in some couple time.

So, yeah, we're raising these kids to work ourselves out of a job. We'll always be their mom and dad. But we're raising them to launch and to fly into their destinies. We're raising men and women. We're raising them to be originals.

THE LAST CURIOUS THREAD

We started our journey with the curious thread that connects us to our children, the umbilical cord that must be cut in order for them to begin independent life. And we've looked at a variety of ways to discover, nurture, and hone the threads woven into our kids—threads that create unique and beautiful purposes. And now there's just one more curious thread to discover.

An oft-repeated Bible verse says, "Like arrows in the hands of a warrior are children born in one's youth" (Psalm 127:4). The construction of arrows is a fascinating process. They have a technology that infuses strength and lightness, feather and stone, the delicacy needed to whittle a shaft and the grit needed to chisel stone into a powerful point. They must be constructed to be accurate, to fly straight and true, to hit the target at which they're aimed.

But for all their sophistication and engineering, arrows are fairly useless without a critical component.

And that component is the bow.

A combination of a curve of wood.

And a curious thread—the bowstring.

The bowstring is tied from one end of the bow to the other. It is the propulsion system for the arrow. Without it, the arrow cannot fly. The bowstring itself needs certain attributes to make it effective. A bowstring must be strong but flexible. It needs to be lightweight. It needs to not be susceptible to the shrinking effects of water, and it needs to stand up well to friction.

Quite a curious thread.

As parents, we replace the connective curious thread of the umbilical cord with the curious thread of the bowstring. We must be strong but flexible in leading our families. We need not drag baggage and regrets and personal insecurities into preparing our kids to fly. We can't shrink back from the floods of life. We must learn to stay unruffled when abrasive people and situations in our lives sand away at our resolve.

We must be the curious thread.

That launches the curious threads in them.

To be arrows of light in a future horizon.

As John W. Whitehead says, "Children are the living messages we send to a time we will not see."

A TREASURE OF WISDOM

Because the conception and gestation and birthing of a book can take a while, my dad has now been gone for many months. Twenty-two days has expanded to over two years. In a way that I could not have planned, I'm currently perched on the lower deck of my brother's lake house in Indiana, a citronella candle flickering ineffectively beside my computer. I'm dancing and wrestling with words, keyboard as percussion, and swatting at mosquitoes, with just enough breeze to make the summer day a contentment.

This is the deck where my dad enjoyed his last days on the lake, his last trip before he would attain eternity.

I'm looking across the water to a shoreline he loved. I'm watching jade green currents softly push north. I'm seeing boats launch into those waters, heading to new destinations and adventures and days.

It all seems an exquisite message.

Because my dad was so intentional about launching and about living, I can hear him now. It's the gift I want to leave for my own kids, that long after I'm gone—long after the heirloom china gets chipped and the silver becomes tarnished—I want them to still hear my voice. To know deeply that I saw them for whom they each are, cherished in their originalities, integral and singular in God's blueprint. To receive a certainty that God placed the threads that define them, with their strengths and quirks and joys and challenges, with specificity and care. To stand at the banks of the river and to have the cloak, the mantle, the blue shirt of love and legacy that will empower them, with God, to part the waters and cross into their destinies. To not be distracted by comparison. To activate. To live. To have the courage to live as an original.

So I'm going to tell them. Again and again. I'm going to show them. Again and again. And I challenge you to do the same. Not just to hand down material stuff but also to entrust something far more valuable, far more precious. To place into their hands a treasure of wisdom that they are the very evidence of an intentional God and that they will launch, they will fly, they will contribute in the great, grand, mysterious epoch that is the divine magnum opus, woven in a chorus of unity with lyrics of harmony, an original song to be sung through the ages.

Since this is the kind of life we have chosen, the life of the Spirit, let us make sure that we do not just hold it as an idea in our heads or a sentiment in our hearts, but work out its implications in every detail of our lives. That means we will not compare ourselves with each other as if one of us were better and another worse. We have far more interesting things to do with our lives. *Each of us is an original.*

Galatians 5:25–26 MSG, *emphasis added*

ACKNOWLEDGMENTS

IT'S ALWAYS BEEN a drive for me, the desire to know the story behind the story, the people behind the curtain, the influences and heart and support behind a project. I listen to the commentary track of movies, I peruse the production credits on an album, and I read the acknowledgments section of a book.

And now I'm writing one. Which is a gorgeous and surreal and deeply cherished experience.

This book has had a long gestation. And there are many who have encouraged me, cheered for me, listened to me wallow in doubt, and feigned interest in all aspects of this work's development, even when it veered to minutiae. You have all been so integral to the realization of this book. And I thank you with deepest gratitude.

- Esther Fedorkevich and the Fedd Agency. You understood and advocated for this message right from the start. That you found a home for this book is a powerful testament to your incomparable persistence and passion. Thank you, thank you, for being such a huge part of bringing to fruition what had long been held in my heart.
- Carolyn McCready and all the amazing HarperCollins/ Zondervan team. You championed this book, cleaned it

up, polished the prose, captured the spirit of the thing, and beautifully tied it up with a bow. And I am awed and grateful.

- Pastor Randy and Denise Phillips and my LifeAustin fellow pastors and family, along with my LifeWomen team. I couldn't be more blessed to work with such an incredible group. You are my people, you are my friends, you are my family. I love you all.

- Jessica Todd, Jennifer Kahla, Andrea Mertz, Kathy Dupuy, Allison Armstrong, Crickett Berlin, Nan Stevens, Cheryl Barnes, Connie and Larry Brown, Diana and Walker Hanson, LeeAnn and Ted Dekker. I bet you're ready to see this thing go to print already so we can talk about something else now. And we will. I promise. Sorry for your tired ears, grateful for your patient and encouraging hearts. Penney Gunn, thank you so much for sharing with me the words "finish the book." You definitely heard clearly from the Lord.

- Jerry and Linda Carr, for the context of the home in which you raised your daughter (Amy and Corbyn VanBrunt, Coleman, Ashton, and Cale) and your son, who would go on to become the great love of my life and the father of my children.

- Bob and Jane Lyles. You raised lifelong learners. You raised readers. You raised curious kids. You raised the bar. And then you launched us. May we live out the legacy you shared, a heritage of Will and Mildred Isom and Allen and Gladys Lyles.

- Dave and Teresa Lyles, Kathryn, Nathan, Claire, Allison, and Lucy. You've watched our parenting from a front row seat for many years and reported back what you saw there. Thank you.

- Rob and Jill Lyles, Clancy, Jack, and Mitchell. From
  the opening imagery of this book from a Paris trip you
  graciously gifted to the closing chapter you allowed me to
  write at the lake house, your fingerprint is all over these
  pages. Lacemaker to launch.
- Madison, McKenna, Justus, Maesyn, Jairus, Journey,
  Merci, and Jake. Your daddy and I have practiced this
  parenting deal on you, real time, the bad and the good.
  I couldn't be more proud of you all, couldn't be more
  delighted at the originals you are. I love you.
- Michael Lloyd Carr, my biggest cheerleader and most
  ardent supporter. You've believed and listened and have
  read and reread passage after passage after passage. At the
  end of the day, this book exists because you held up my
  arms. Thank you. I love you more.

NOTES

1. "Households and Families: 2010," *2010 Census Briefs*, United States Census Bureau, April 2012, https://www.census.gov/prod/cen2010/briefs/c2010br-14.pdf
2. http://www.aljazeera.com/indepth/features/2013/12/south-korean-students-wracked-with-stress-201312884628494144.html
3. https://www.bostonglobe.com/metro/2015/03/16/suicide-rate-mit-higher-than-national-average/1aGWr7lRjiEyhoD1WIT78I/story.html
4. Amanda Ripley, *The Smartest Kids in the World and How They Got That Way* (New York: Simon & Schuster Paperbacks, 2013), 5.
5. http://newsinfo.iu.edu/web/page/normal/6073.html
6. http://www.dailymail.co.uk/news/article-2098473/Wanda-Holloway-s-daughter-Shanna-breaks-silence-Texas-Cheerleading-murder-plot.html
7. http://digitalscholarship.unlv.edu/cgi/viewcontent.cgi?article=2333&context=thesesdissertations
8. http://www.psychologytoday.com/blog/compassion-matters/201304/the-dangers-narcissistic-parents
9. https://growtheroses.wordpress.com/tag/blessed-zelie-martin
10. http://onlinelibrary.wiley.com/doi/10.1111/j.1467–6494.2007.00480.x/abstract
11. http://education-consumers.org/issues-public-education-research-analysis/childrens-behavioral-styles

12. http://www.census.gov/newsroom/press-releases/2014/cb14 –224.html
13. http://classroom.synonym.com/extracurricular-activities -academic-grades-4906.html
14. http://www.beliefnet.com/columnists/moviemom/2011/09/ interview-david-code-on-how-parental-stress-is-toxic-for-kids .html#ixzz3Zs4KK1Mh
15. Celine Martin, *The Mother of the Little Flower* (Charlotte: TAN Books, Reissue, 2005).